P9-DEW-135

Lucian Freud

BOOKS BY PHOEBE HOBAN

Basquiat: A Quick Killing in Art
Alice Neel: The Art of Not Sitting Pretty

Lucian Freud

EYES WIDE OPEN

PHOEBE HOBAN

ICONS SERIES

New Harvest
Houghton Mifflin Harcourt
BOSTON • NEW YORK
2014

Copyright © 2014 by Phoebe Hoban

All rights reserved

This edition published by special arrangement with Amazon Publishing

For information about permission to reproduce selections
from this book, go to www.apub.com.

www.hmhco.com

Library of Congress Cataloging-in-Publication Data
Hoban, Phoebe.
Lucian Freud : eyes wide open / Phoebe Hoban.
pages cm. — (Icons series)
ISBN 978-0-544-11459-3 (hardback)
1. Freud, Lucian. 2. Painters — Great Britain — Biography. I. Title.
ND497.F75H63 2014
759.2 — dc23
[B]
2013042031

Printed in the United States of America
DOC 10 9 8 7 6 5 4 3 2 1

For my parents,
Lillian Hoban
and
Russell Hoban

Contents

Lucian Freud

The Art of Looking

I MAGINE A YOUNG man walking across a high, slender wooden beam, eyes tightly closed. It's a striking image, but one Lucian Freud would never paint. As his cousin Carola Zentner recalled from a long-past summer in the Freuds' country house, "There was an oak beam which went from one side of the barn to the other, twenty feet in length at least, and about nine inches wide. And I have a distinct memory of Lucian, about fifteen, walking in a rather languid way up the stairs, and then closing his eyes and walking across the beam. It was impressive."

Although such bravura abandon would characterize much of his later life, as an artist Lucian Freud never closed his eyes. His omnivorous scrutiny bordered on obsessive; his forensic curiosity was satisfied only through countless sittings, as if by minutely examining and recording the world in his studio, he could command it. His gaze has been called "cruel." More accurately, it was insatiable.

Where did Lucian learn to look at things the way he did? It would be easy to attribute his particular form of acute observation to genetics: his grandfather, after all, was Sigmund Freud, the father of psychoanalysis. It is almost impossible to write about Lucian Freud without drawing a parallel between Sigmund's repeated sessions with his patients and Lucian's repeated sessions with his subjects. Both took place in a private room, with a recumbent figure being intently examined, although Sigmund's focus was the unseen, and Lucian's the seen.

Indeed, Sigmund Freud's study, which Lucian visited as a child at his grandfather's house at Berggasse 19, in Vienna, and which was later recreated, objet d'art by objet d'art, in 1938, in a townhouse in London at 20 Maresfield Gardens (now the Freud Museum, London), not only provided an influential working template; it was replete with key imagery that would resurface in Lucian Freud's paintings: ceramic and bronze heads; horses (a deep and life-long love — one of his earliest works is a sandstone sculpture of a three-legged horse); and a rich array of Egyptian antiquities, including mummy portraits, whose flat aspect he later emulated. One of Lucian's favorite books was J. H. Breasted's *Geschichte Aegyptens,* which was given to him when he was sixteen. Freud even depicted it in several pieces: *Still Life with Book* (1993), *The Egyptian Book* (1994).

The architect Richard Neutra, a friend of Lucian's father, Ernst, recalled Sigmund Freud's study in detail: "Pompeian frescoes ... mummy fragments ... many Egyptian bronzes ... ceramics ... antique vases, paintings ... sculptures ... Greek gold ornaments and these books ... the erotic work. Terrific."

In a short film clip in the Freud Museum's archives, Lucian, age fifteen, can be seen, as he stands side by side with his grandfather (who died the next year) near a goldfish pond at 39 Elsworthy Road, where Sigmund stayed until the house at Maresfield Gardens was ready. Lucian was extremely fond of Sigmund — and later flamboyantly wore his grandfather's fur-trimmed greatcoat around London. He refused to go to the funeral, causing a family scene. "Doing so would have been absolutely meaningless to me," he told writer John Gruen in the 1970s.

Even at that early age, Lucian was considered a wunderkind. "I met him first in the winter of 1938–39 and [he was] already spoken of as a boy wonder," wrote one of his first chroniclers,

Lawrence Gowing. "He was in a studio flat in Charlotte Street, round the corner from the house where Rimbaud and Verlaine took rooms, in company with a self-appointed Svengali who showed him off, whispering behind his hand, 'Marvellous.'"

And something else, less tangible. He was also, notes Gowing, "fly [*sic*], perceptive, lithe, and with a hint of menace," characteristics which would remain lifelong traits. This slightly sinister quality was also observed by Stephen Spender, one of the first to reproduce Freud's work, who thought of him as "totally alive, like something not entirely human, a leprechaun, a changeling child, or if there is a male opposite, a witch."

It was not only Lucian's "extraordinary looks," remarked on by the artist's friend Bruce Bernard in his authoritative monograph on Freud, that made a striking impression, but what Gowing describes as "the pointed intensity apparent even in Freud's juvenile vision." That pointed intensity would be Freud's leitmotif.

Lucian Michael Freud was born in Berlin on December 8, 1922. (His middle name refers to an archangel, as do those of his two brothers, Stephen Gabriel and Clement Raphael.) His father was Sigmund's youngest son and fourth child, Ernst, thought of by the family as a *Gluckskind*, or lucky child. Although Ernst had originally wanted to be an artist (at least so Sigmund told his famous patient, the "Wolf Man," in a discussion of his son's career), he decided on the more pragmatic profession of architecture. But he remained steeped in the arts. According to Gowing, who saw a series of his 1913 Alpine landscapes, Ernst was an accomplished watercolorist. And like many German youths, he was an ardent fan of the poet Rainer Maria Rilke, so much so that Sigmund wrote his dear friend Lou Andreas-Salomé (famously Rilke's lover and mentor), asking if she could arrange a meeting between Rilke and his son. Rilke returned the compliment by sending Ernst a book of poems,

Field Sermon, by his friend Regina Ullmann, which he personally inscribed. Ernst eventually did meet the poet in Vienna, in February of 1916, when the young soldier was at home on leave from the army.

Lucian's mother, after whom he was named, was Lucie Brasch, the daughter of a prosperous Berlin corn merchant, Joseph Brasch, and his wife Elise. Lucie studied classical philology in Munich, as well as art history with the famous Swiss art historian Heinrich Wölfflin for a year in Munich, after first reading German studies in Berlin. Zentner, the daughter of Lucie's older sister, Gerda, describes Lucie as "tremendously vibrant and vivacious, an intellectual. She had done classics at university, which was fairly unusual when she was a young girl. She was very funny and very beautiful, with jet black hair." As for her background, "Lucie's father was the president of the Corn Exchange in those days. It was a Buddenbrooks sort of family." (As Clement Freud put it in his memoir, *Freud Ego,* "My father's family was distinguished, my mother's was rich.")

Ernst first attended the Technical University (Technische Hochschule) in Vienna from 1912 to 1913, studying mathematics, engineering, and sketching after nature and the body, among other courses. In 1913, he left Vienna for Munich, where he studied architecture with Theodor Fischer at the Technical University (Technische Hochschule) in Munich, and, according to Gowing, also took an art course. He volunteered to fight for the Austrian-Hungarian army in 1914. Although at first he was rejected for health reasons, he was eventually assigned to a gun unit at Doberdoplateau, which came under heavy attack, leaving him the only survivor. He was awarded a gold medal (he eventually earned three) and an architectural commission to commemorate five fallen fellow soldiers.

Freud had not dropped out of university to join the army, and when the war was over, he returned to his studies in late 1918. He also met Lucie Brasch, who was at the time studying in Munich. Ernst passed his final exams in 1919, and his first job out of school was as an intern with the architect Fritz Landauer. But later that year he moved to Berlin to join Lucie, who had returned to her family's home after finishing her studies.

The year 1920 did not begin well for Ernst. His sister, Sophie, died on January 25 from influenza, and Ernst was involved in the design of her gravestone. Around that time, he himself developed a lung ailment, and was prescribed a stay at a sanitarium in Arosa, Switzerland. He was well enough to marry Lucie in Berlin on May 18, 1920. However, he was forced to return to the sanitarium for three months from February through April 1921. His son's health was of some concern to Sigmund, who wrote to a friend that the sanitarium sojourn was "so short after one has married into a rich family. . . . I only hope that the Braschs are too refined to suspect anything behind this." But by then, Lucie was pregnant with her first son, Stephen Gabriel Freud, born that July.

At the time, the couple was living in what was recalled as a "charming home" located on Regentstrasse, in the well-to-do Tiergarten quarter. When Lucian was two years old, a third son, Clement, was born, necessitating a move to a larger apartment, on the same street, Number 23 Regentstrasse. (Clement Freud refers to the neighborhood as the "best part of Berlin.") The family lived there until Lucian was eight years old. Its interior and furnishings, designed by Ernst, merited a 1928 article and photograph in *Die Pyramide* magazine.

In his book, *Ernst L. Freud, Architect,* Volker M. Welter gives a detailed description of this home, with its many modern elements and close attention to detail. As Welter describes it, Freud's designs made use of sophisticated notions of decoration, functionality, and domesticity. There was a studio/living room that contained cubic furniture; a wall-to-wall bookshelf built around a brick fireplace along with a de Stijl magazine cupboard; and Ernst's desk, with its open, built-in shelves. Large boxy chairs, facing the fireplace and paired with the desk, completed the picture. The bedrooms, in contrast, were made of light-colored, delicate lacquered wood. The wardrobes had glazed doors with curtained glass panes. This same furniture was later shipped to the Freuds' new London home when the family fled Germany.

Lucian, who, like his mother, was nicknamed Lux, was exposed to art from an early age. The family house was hung with prints by Hokusai and Dürer. Sigmund, who was "marvelously understanding and amused" by Lucian's interest in art, also gave him material, including prints of *The Seasons* by Bruegel and an illustrated copy of *The Arabian Nights,* and they were both fans of an early German comic strip, *Max and Moritz.*

The children had a governess and a nursery well-furnished with books and toys. Lucian remembered a favorite jointed wooden horse, which, he later said, helped him understand "the mechanical attachment of ligaments to bone."

According to Carola Zentner, "What I can tell you quite clearly is that Ernst, being an architect, and being a good middle-class Jew, surrounded himself with beautiful objects, and was well-informed about the artistic world around him. Ernst also had quite a bit of Egyptology in his study. I remember in my childhood being trailed around museums endlessly, and I suspect the same would have held true for Lucian." Indeed, Lucian's maternal grandmother often took him to the Egyptian Museum in Berlin, where he was mesmerized by the head of Queen Nefertiti.

Berlin at the time was the capital of the newly formed Weimar Republic. Ernst Freud, whose influences included the Viennese architect Adolf Loos, set up office at home, and briefly collaborated with another architect, Alexander Kurz, also from Vienna. Among the firm's projects were two semi-detached houses and a tobacco warehouse. Ernst readily found connections and clients among his father's friends and those of Lucie's family, designing "bourgeois" domestic interiors and becoming, according to his biographer, Welter, something of a "society architect." Clement Freud wrote that his father belonged to the "Bauhaus school of architecture, and designed houses for famous clients." Ernst created innovative modern homes ranging from an urban dwelling for a psychoanalyst couple to a huge country home for Dr. Theodore Frank, a director of the Deutsche Bank.

Even more important, Berlin was developing into a center for psychoanalysis, and Ernst became known for his designs of psychoanalytic studies and offices, a specialty he continued with success after emigrating to London. He even designed the eminent British analyst Melanie Klein's consulting room, one of his first projects there. (Ernst's consulting rooms, unlike Sigmund's study, tended to be sleek and geometric to the point of starkness, but he maintained Sigmund's spatial equation of couch to chair.) The Freud family was affluent enough to have servants: a maid, a cook, and a governess, as well as a summer house on the Baltic Sea. Located on the island of Hiddensee, known as a plush bohemian enclave, this vacation home was actually half of a turn-of-the-century fisherman's cottage that Ernst had embellished by raising the roof, covering it with tiles instead of thatch, and adding two dormer windows and a sliding glass door.

Ernst's aesthetic refinement was apparent in all his designs, from the built-in furniture in one client's nursery to a unique table at Hiddensee, made of brass and inset with a "wonderful material, rubber, kind of greeny white with bits of red and black," still remembered in precise detail by Carola Zentner. Ernst shared with Sigmund (and also with Rilke) a profound sense of the emotional value of the individual objects chosen to adorn a room or home — its household gods. Lucian's keenly developed sense of the intimate sanctity of his working space, his studio, was something he probably inherited not only from his grandfather, but from his father.

Although Lucian and his brothers were not brought up to observe Judaism (Clement Freud says he didn't even learn he was Jewish until he was six, since, as his cousin Carola explained, "We were Germans before we were Jews"), Ernst Freud had a strong early Zionist connection. When he was a student in Vienna, Freud became a member of a Zionist youth organization, an activity he continued when he moved to Munich and Berlin. He became close friends with a Zionist named Gustav Krojanker, who later was a director of Judischer Verlag, a publishing house, and he designed some furniture for him. At one point, Ernst even delivered a lecture on "Radical Zionism."

Ernst and Lucie subscribed to *Der Jude* (a Zionist magazine), copies of which were on the shelves of Lucian's childhood home. Ernst's Zionist acquaintances, some of whom he knew through Sigmund, also provided him with commissions. Max Eitingon, a doctor and one of the first Freudian psychoanalysts, hired him to design the interior of his apartment, as well as giving him his first realized commission: the interior of Berlin's Policlinic for the Psychoanalytic Treatment of Nervous Diseases (according to Welter, the world's first psychoanalytic clinic). Through Eitingon, Ernst was introduced to the Zionist architect Alexander Baerwald, who built the Technion in Haifa. Ernst was supposed to be employed by Baerwald to help create plans for an oil refinery to be built in Palestine. In the late 1920s, Ernst was also engaged to do the early drawings for a house for Chaim and Vera Weizmann, to be built on Mount Scopus. Neither project was ever realized, although Ernst did the drawings. (The house was eventually built in Rehovot, near the Weizman Institute, by Erich Mendelsohn.) There even seem to have been some nascent plans for Ernst to move to Palestine to help build Hebrew University. In the 1930s, he designed the office and furniture for the banker Richard Ginsberg, another Zionist contact from Ernst's student days. (Ernst moved in illustrious circles: on one social occasion at his home, he introduced Sigmund to Albert Einstein.)

As Jews, Ernst and his family were forced to flee Berlin with Adolf Hitler's rise to power in 1933; Lucie had already experienced a painful incident of anti-Semitism the summer before at their Hiddensee house, when a neighbor verbally accosted her and her sons. The urgent situation hit even closer to home when Lucie's brother-in-law (and Carola and Lucian's uncle) Rudy Mosse, a landowner and member of a prominent newspaper family, was, according to Zentner, "arrested at five in the morning and marched off, minus shoelaces and braces, and given to understand what was awaiting him. He was killed there and then, within hours. I have heard he was either thrown under a tram or he was shot."

Lucian had strong recollections of those dark days. He said he saw the Reichstag fire, in February 1933, although he also told Gowing that his school, Französisches Gymnasium, had made the young students take a detour in order to spare them the sight of the parliament building burning. He even claimed to have seen and photographed Hitler himself. "I was nine, in 1931. I was walking around with my governess and I had a camera with me. I was fascinated by him because he had huge bodyguards and he was really very small," he told one interviewer.

According to Gruen, as early as 1929, Lucian was "exposed to schoolmates eagerly mimicking their elders in 'games' of looting, lighting of fires and placing ominous symbols on the walls." He saw Jews being jeered at, and "fell victim to fears he had never encountered before. The effect of these notorious circumstances marked him for life." Still, Lucian later had to be stopped from emulating his schoolmates and drawing swastikas. He also once asked his mother why Jews were superior to others, and was told, "Because they don't kill people," a concept Lucian told Bruce Bernard he didn't totally apprehend. "Being Jewish, I never think about it, yet it's a part of me," he would later tell one of his most famous subjects, the performance artist Leigh Bowery. In any case, the family left Germany just days before a public book burning of the works of Jewish intellectuals, including Sigmund Freud.

As Lucian himself put it in an interview, "What kind of boy was I? Well, I had a very conventional childhood in Berlin. Then, around 1929, I became aware of being a Jew. Suddenly, one was an outsider, someone to be hunted down. I rebelled, of course, and became very resentful. I would disappear from home, and let no one know where I was. I was very secretive, and would drive my parents wild. Anyway, in 1932 [*sic*], we came to England."

Ernst went on an exploratory mission first, in June, establishing a home and contacts, and writing to Lucie frequently, describing his meetings, both serendipitous and otherwise, with other Jewish exiles and with several of his father's friends. He also met with architects for prospective work, including Francis Rowland Yerbury, the secretary of the Architectural Association, and Serge Chermayeff, the architect Eric Mendelsohn's British business partner. That September, Lucie and their three sons left Berlin for London, with Ernst, who had returned to Berlin, following them in November. They were relieved when a specially designed marble table, its tubular leg stuffed with "the Freud fortune," arrived from Berlin soon afterwards; they had only been legally allowed to take a small sum of money with them.

Not surprisingly, many of Ernst's early clients in London were also German-Jewish refugees. Thus he was quickly able to emulate his Berlin practice in his new city, creating designs that ranged from the music room of Pine House in Surrey to the renovation of the Hampstead home of a psychiatrist (complete with a mural of Diana among wild animals) to the Frognal Close project, a multitownhouse development.

As for his own home, for their initial year or so in London, Ernst and Lucie and their three sons occupied several apartments, first on Clarges Street near Piccadilly, in Westminster, and then in Hampstead. But by 1935, they had moved to what would become the family's permanent abode, 32 St. John's Terrace, reminiscent in some ways of their old Berlin neighborhood. This three-story house was novel for its extreme narrowness; it was just fifteen and a half feet wide. Ernst quickly set about renovating the place, creating a large living room and dining area on the first floor, with a built-in sideboard. His study was to the rear of the ground floor, with glass sliding doors opening onto a garden. The house was furnished with other familiar items from their Berlin apartment, including pieces in the master bedroom on the second floor as well as in Lucian and his brothers' bedrooms. Freud's study featured a fireplace, which, like the one in their Berlin place, had wraparound bookshelves; the screen was from Berlin. The overall effect was one of modernity and efficiency, somewhat antithetical to the standard London apartment of the time.

Over the next few years, a number of Freud family relatives moved nearby. After Sigmund's death, Alexander Freud purchased property there, and Anna Freud and an associate opened various Hampstead war nurseries not far from Maresfield Gardens, which was close to St. John's Wood, eventually transforming the neighborhood into a kind of Freud family enclave, or as Welter puts it (referring to Sigmund Freud's Vienna address), a "Berggassen quarter."

Ernst also created a wonderful British surrogate for the Freud family's lost seaside cottage in Hiddensee. Ernst bought and renovated a thatched cottage in Walberswick, a small town on the coast of Suffolk, on the North Sea. They called their new holiday home Hidden House, perhaps after Hiddensee. Ernst added a large, beautiful bay window to the tall, one-story building, which had a barn-like main room that was open to the rafters. It was there, one summer day, that Carola Zentner saw her teenage cousin Lucian tightrope-walking across the ceiling beam with his eyes closed.

Learning to Be Lucian

L UCIAN BEGAN DRAWING at a very young age; one of his earliest extant works is the disturbing *Chimneys on Fire,* a crayon drawing of nine similarly colored houses with bright red flames streaming from their chimneys, done in 1928, when he was six. Then there is the 1930 crayon drawing of five birds, done at Hiddensee, that his mother submitted to the Peggy Guggenheim gallery, where it was shown in a children's drawing show in 1938. Although she kept drawings by all three boys, and even a few pieces by Ernst, that Lucie saved the drawing by her seven-year-old son for so many decades is testament to her conviction, from a very young age, of his brilliance. (Not to mention Lucian's own conviction. "This is good, take care of it," he wrote on one.)

Lucie seemed to favor Lucian. As Clement Freud recalled, "My mother was very beautiful and fairly distant. When she came into the nursery, she nodded to Stephen and me, and sat down with Lucian and whispered. They had secrets." As Freud later put it, "From very early on she treated me, in a way, as an only child. I resented her interest." Zentner recalls seeing Lucian's drawings proudly displayed in the Freuds' home. As the art historian and critic William Feaver noted, "From childhood there were drawings of goblins and fairies, tables piled high and the pear tree outside the Freuds' holiday home on the Baltic island of Hiddensee. Later came fantastical *jeux d'esprit,* sharp im-

ages of friends patient enough to sit for him, etchings and drawings demonstrating his love of Ingres." (And, always, pictures of
horses and dogs.)

Soon after their arrival in London, Lucian and his brothers, Clement and Stephen, were shipped off to Dartington,
a progressive co-ed boarding school in Devon sympathetic to
the teachings of Sigmund Freud, so much so that Ernst was not
charged tuition for his three sons. There, Lucian preferred riding horses to going to art class (he didn't like the teacher) and
soon established himself as something of a wild child. From
an early age, he displayed a much greater affinity with animals
than with people. (In Berlin, the family had a greyhound named
Billy, perhaps the prototype of the adult Freud's beloved — and
much painted — whippets.) Remarking on his unsocial behavior, his father once introduced him as "this wild animal, my
son."

Freud later said of the family's move to London, "Hitler's attitude to the Jews persuaded my father to bring us to London,
the place I prefer in every way to anywhere I've been." But the
transition could hardly have been easy for a ten-year-old boy,
starting with the English language itself.

Indeed, Lucian, who at the time could not speak or read
English, and was also left-handed, had difficulty learning to
write it in proper cursive script, developing an idiosyncratic
hand and retaining throughout his life a slightly German-in-
flected accent. "When I came to England first I could only do
German-gothic handwriting," he told Feaver. And, according
to a letter from Dartington Hall, "Lucian doesn't seem to have
mastered the English language but is fast forgetting all his German; this seems to be quite a good argument against his taking
up French." (Lucian was not alone in his difficulty with English.
Clement recalled being initially tormented by not understanding the new language.)

Located in rural Devon, Dartington had a farm, and it was there that Lucian could usually be found, "tending horses and goats." He was already well-acquainted with horses from time spent at his maternal grandparents' estate in Kotbus, until the stables burned down, creating a vivid memory of "rampaging animals," perhaps the inspiration for an extraordinary linocut, *Runaway Horse,* he did at age fourteen. At Dartington, where he remained for two years, his love of horses was such that he considered becoming a jockey. His brother recalls that he "excelled at riding, having no fear." He often slept in the stables "with my favorite horses," and took unofficial possession of a pony named Starlight. Still, that didn't prevent Lucian from throwing stones at the horses, because he loved to see them gallop. (When a teacher tried to stop him, Lucian ran off, according to Clement, who describes his brother at the time as "fearless, curly-haired, belligerent and artistic.")

Lucian's violence extended to his schoolmates; he "hit them, wrestled them to the ground, gave and got black eyes and bloody noses." Lucian also apparently had a wily side. During school holidays, he made pocket change by selling packets of Players Navy Cut cigarettes cadged from the machine in their building on Clarges Street, which he had discovered would accept half-penny coins instead of the required shilling.

When Dartington informed his parents that they "could not put up with him any more," Lucian was sent to the prep school of Bryanston, an all-boys school, where he still caused enough trouble to be frequently disciplined, not by corporal punishment but by mandatory long-distance running, something he thoroughly enjoyed. He was eventually asked to leave that school for his "disruptive influence on the community," including an incident that scandalized the proper locals; Lucian dropped his trousers in a street on Bournemouth on a dare from a friend. But it was at Bryanston, in 1937, that Lucian created a remarkable artwork, primitive yet precociously evocative: a three-legged horse sculpted from sandstone by the then fifteen-year-old student.

Ernst used the horse as evidence of his son's unique talent, and was able to win a place for him at the Central Arts and Crafts School in London in 1938, where he eschewed life-drawing classes with the well-regarded Bernard Meninsky, but briefly studied sculpture with John Skeaping. It is possibly in his class that Lucian made "a small alabaster fish lying on a rock" that Sigmund Freud gave to his beloved student, Princess Marie Bonaparte, in the hopes that she would become Lucian's patron, which she later did.

But Freud had not changed his unruly ways, and he managed to last for only one term, learning to play Ping-Pong and becoming an habitué of such Soho hangouts as the baroque Café Royal and the racy Coffee An. According to Lucian, it was at this point that his life "really began." At Coffee An, he learned in passing from a young female companion about Cedric Morris's East Anglian School of Painting and Drawing in Essex. (Freud later painted her: *Girl on the Quay,* 1941.)

Meanwhile, Sigmund Freud had finally been driven out of Vienna, arriving in London on June 6, 1938. Such was the concern for Freud when the Nazis marched into Vienna that the American ambassador and Princess Marie Bonaparte actually moved into his Berggasse apartment to protect him, according to Clement. That did not prevent the SS from damaging a few things, refusing to wipe their boots when asked, and forcing Freud to sign a document, to which he added the postscript: "I would like to recommend the SS to everyone." He and his wife Martha left Vienna on the Orient Express on June 4, along with their household staff and a doctor. They got to Paris the following day, where Ernst met them, and spent the day with Princess Marie Bonaparte before traveling to London on the night boat. They arrived at Victoria Station on June 6.

Freud, Martha, and Anna had temporary lodgings until they could settle into 20 Maresfield Gardens, Hampstead, in the two-story, brick, Queen Anne Revival-style townhouse that Ernst had found for them, and which he soon renovated. He tore down walls, and added a balcony and loggia. Although an effort was made to duplicate the most important element of Berggasse 19, Freud's beloved study, the basic layout made that architecturally impossible. However, great care was taken to insure that many objects from his Viennese study found their place in the new space, accomplished by installing a floor-to-ceiling bookcase that included two Biedermeier display cases from Vienna, and adding other display cases and a handsome farm table on which antique carvings and statues were thoughtfully arranged. Freud's psychoanalytic couch was placed against the wall, with a chair behind it. Clement recalls visiting his grandfather every Sunday, with other family members, Lucian among them. Thanks to a film clip made by Princess Marie Bonaparte on Saturday, June 25, soon after Freud's move to London, as well as several photographs, it is clear that Lucian spent time with his grandfather, and that he would have had the opportunity to reacquaint himself with his fascinating collection of antiquities.

Sigmund Freud died on September 23, 1939, just fifteen months after moving to London. Lucian was the only immediate family member not to attend his funeral. "There was a sort of hole in his cheek like a brown apple; that was why there was no death mask made, I imagine," he later said. "I was upset." Three days after his death, Freud's body was cremated at Golders Green Crematorium, located in the Jewish section of London. His ashes were placed in an ancient Greek urn that Freud had been given by Princess Marie Bonaparte and that had once adorned his study.

Britain and France had declared war on Germany just three weeks earlier. According to Clement, Lucian occasionally attended the Slade art school (although he is the only one to place

him there at that time.) John Richardson would meet him there
a few years later, in 1942. When women on the street would ask
Lucian and Clement—who along with the rest of the Freud
family had just become naturalized citizens—why they were
not enlisted, Lucian's stock response was, "Madame, why aren't
you having a war baby?"

By autumn 1939, Lucian Freud finally made a serious effort
to study art. Earlier that summer, following the tip from his
Coffee An friend, he had enrolled in Cedric Morris's school in
East Anglia, Dedham, Essex (the East Anglian School of Painting and Drawing), where he was mentored by the odd if influential Morris. It was around this time that Freud received a copy
of J. H. Breasted's *Geschichte Aegyptens,* published in Vienna in
1936. With its images of ancient mummy portraits and sculpted
heads, it would inspire and inform his work throughout his career. The book was given to him possibly by his father, Ernst,
or so Gowing wrote. Given the timing, it might even have belonged to Sigmund himself, who cited it as a source in *Moses
and Monotheism,* published shortly before his death. (Freud
told Feaver he couldn't remember if he got it from his father or
from Peter Watson, an early patron.)

In the charismatic Morris, who along with his lover, Arthur
Lett-Haines, had founded the school, Freud met something of
a kindred spirit, someone who seemed as untrammeled as himself. More important, he finally learned to focus on his work,
inspired by Morris's unconventional method. "He worked in a
very odd way. Used to start at the top and then go down, like
a tapestry maker, from top to bottom as if he were unrolling
something that was actually there. . . . Great to watch. Gave a
feeling of sureness," he told Feaver. Freud's admiration of Morris
(who was also a horticulturist) and satisfaction in having landed
in a place "where people were working seriously and there was
a very strong atmosphere" did not prevent him from his usual
shenanigans. Lucian claimed responsibility for burning the

place down by being careless with a cigarette; he and a friend had been smoking in a studio the night before. (Like many artists before and since, he cultivated his image as an enfant terrible, and this anecdote has become a classic.)

After the school was incinerated, Freud stayed with Morris at his home, a pink farmhouse in Benton End, Hadleigh, Suffolk. Morris was one of a circle of prominent gay men who mentored and promoted the young Freud. When the Freud family moved for a time, in 1939, from St. John's Wood to Hampstead, they were downstairs neighbors of the poet Stephen Spender, who was an early fan of Freud's, and clearly sensed his singularity. Spender once recalled that when his wife, Natasha, was sick, Lucian came upstairs to offer her solace in the form of one asparagus stalk. Spender was the first to publish Freud's work, a "self-portrait," in April 1940, when he was just seventeen, in the magazine *Horizon,* founded by Peter Watson and edited by Cyril Connolly.

As Bernard observed, "Freud became involved with the important homosexual stratum in British cultural life." This included Morris, Watson, and arguably Spender, who was bisexual. Freud quickly understood that these were the major supporters of the avant-garde, and he directly benefitted from being taken under their wing. Morris, who painted a remarkable portrait of Freud at nineteen, with intense blue eyes; voluptuous red lips; and a head of rich, dark curls, certainly influenced Freud's first serious work, both in terms of style and subject.

Morris (actually Sir Cedric Morris, the ninth baronet of Clasemont), was well-known, both as a horticulturist — he cultivated a four-acre garden at Suffolk — and for his botanical paintings (mostly of plants from his own garden), as well as pictures of landscapes and birds. He painted pigeons, herons, and sparrow hawks, as would Lucian, who like his teacher, often used botanical images in his art. Morris also did portraits, characterized by large-eyed, caricature-like figures. While at

Morris's, Freud painted *Box of Apples in Wales* (1939), a fairly traditional oil to which he later added some Welsh mountains, from a trip he took to Wales that fall, with a fellow student, David Kentish. They were briefly joined by Stephen Spender, who gave Freud a blank publisher's dummy to draw in, and asked him to illustrate the novel he was working on, *The Backward Son.* As he wrote in a letter to Morris, "I've finished my picture of a crate of apples by putting a Welsh landscape in the background.... I also painted a large monster and landscapes and more monsters and a street at night.... I am doing a great deal of drawing all the time. I think my painting is getting much better and the paint is much more interesting than it used to be."

Of Lucian at the time, Spender wrote, "Lucian is the most intelligent person I have met since I first knew Auden at Oxford.... He looks like Harpo Marx and is amazingly talented, and also wise...." (The following year, Freud would paint Spender at 20 Maresfield Gardens, where the poet was then living.)

Lucian's self-portrait was published in *Horizon,* in April 1940, and he got his first newspaper notice, in the London *Evening Standard,* which wrote that the artist "promises to be a remarkable painter ... intelligent and imaginative with an instinctive rather than a scientific psychological sense."

Paintings of that year include two rather expressionistic works, *Horses and a Figure,* and *Woman with Reflected Suitors.* (Both have an almost Munch-like quality, although Freud later vehemently voiced his disdain for German expressionism.) *Memory of London,* a portrait of a sinister-looking corner newspaperman, bleakly evokes the city in wartime. His mesmerizing self-portrait, much less flattering than the painting Morris did of him, displays the flat, illustrative aspect and emphasized eyes of much of Freud's work for the next few years. In it, his face is oddly rippled, perhaps because he painted it from his reflection in a mirror (something he would do many times in later years).

His portrait of Morris (1940) shows his teacher with a pipe, a thin, eccentric figure with one eye mysteriously blackened. Other works of the time include nimble pen drawings of Cyril Connolly and Stephen Spender. His antic 1940 *Landscape with Birds* could be an illustration in a scary children's book, and probably was influenced by the sixteenth-century German artist Matthias Grünewald, whose work he admired. It shows a boy who is undoubtedly Lucian, despite the fact that his face is black, prancing to the point of levitation above a landscape that includes the ocean and a sea wall. Above him, in a cloud-quilted sky, are ten demented-looking birds with straggly, feathered wings, whom Bruce Bernard describes as "falling from the sky."

In the winter of 1941, using money he won for a textile design, Lucian suddenly left for Liverpool and enlisted in the Merchant Navy, as an ordinary seaman on the SS *Baltrover*. Although he packed his paints and art supplies, the cold (rags placed in a bucket instantly froze) and the danger (a boat directly behind his was bombed, and his own convoy was attacked by air and submarine) prevented him from doing much more than tattooing a few of his fellow sailors.

But three months later, after one transatlantic crossing to Halifax, Nova Scotia, and back, Lucian's sailing days were over. He came down with tonsillitis and was hospitalized, an episode he depicted in a sorrowful painting, *Hospital Ward* (1941), of a young man in bed (a conflation of himself and Peter Watson), a uniformed nurse and several other bedridden invalids in the background. When he left the hospital, he returned to Morris's school, which had been reestablished in Suffolk.

Freud described Morris's work as "revealing in a way which was almost improper," and Lucian emulated him, to a certain degree. His parents were appalled by the results. Ernst wrote to Morris, "We are interested to hear that you are delighted with his progress ... I could not help but loathe the last picture he brought to London but his style and his subjects will as I hope change."

Lucian was still evolving his own style, but for now his work retained the flat aspect and enlarged eyes typical both of Morris's work and of German caricature (which Lucian considered to be an insult) with a nod to surrealism (there had been a big surrealist show in London in 1936), as in his dismal-looking *The Refugees* (1941), which hung in the *Horizon* offices, a "joke group" that had as its centerpiece a local dentist in dark glasses, surrounded by his family, including a goblin-like child sticking out a pointed tongue. This style reached its apotheosis in *The Village Boys* (1942); the central figure is reminiscent of his own self-portrait, and the background is cluttered with some of the paintings Freud had in his studio at Morris's school in Benton End.

A notable characteristic of Lucian's work even then is its obsessive attention to detail. His *Man and Town* (1940–41), featuring the large figure of a man in front of a village with literally hundreds of tiny, individually detailed houses behind him, is a case in point. (Its level of minutiae is so extreme it recalls some examples of Outsider art.) Carola Zentner observed in awe as Lucian did an incredibly detailed drawing of an infant girl, seemingly rendering each hair of her toy monkey's fur (*Juliet Moore, Asleep,* 1943). "I even now remember very well tiptoeing up and standing behind him, and watching him. He was doing a pen and ink drawing of a baby in a laundry basket with a toy monkey, and the amazingly intricate basket weave that made up the basket. And I remember thinking to myself, *Unbelievable.*"

Peter Watson played a key role in this period of Lucian Freud's life, by becoming his first patron and setting up Freud and the painter John Craxton in a studio at 14 Abercorn Place in St. John's Wood. Freud briefly took a life class at Goldsmith's College in New Cross during this time, and had his drawings exhibited in his first show, at London's Lefevre gallery in 1942.

John Richardson, who became a long-term friend of the painter, first met Lucian during the Blitz in 1942 at the Slade School, where "he had materialized" to "check us out" (also checking out the young woman with the "dead-white face" that Richardson intended to marry). He arranged to meet Freud a few months later at the Café Royal in London, and many years later vividly described his impression of the then twenty-year-old rising star: "One wartime evening, I remember seeing Lucian at the center of a greenery-yallery group, as thin and sharp-profiled as a cutout, standing on one leg like a stork, his eyes lowered in intense wariness. 'Dear boy, who is that Rimbaud look-alike,' one old poetaster drawled to a fellow. 'Young Freud at it again,' was the reply."

3

Women and Muses

THE YEAR 1943 began a formative period in Freud's life; his work matured into his signature early illustrative style and, while he was still living at Abercorn Place, he met the first great love of his life, the extraordinary Lorna Wishart. He would later describe her to Gowing as "the first person who meant something to me" — in an incestuous twist, he would go on to marry her niece, Kitty Garman.

A remarkable femme fatale, ten years his senior, Lorna had wed Ernest Wishart, son of Sir Sidney Wishart, the Sheriff of London, when she was only sixteen, having seduced him when she was fourteen. She bore the first of her two sons, Michael, when she was seventeen. By all accounts, Lorna Wishart was a bewitching creature, from her throaty voice to her deep blue eyes to her indomitable spunk. She was also glamorous, drenched in jewels and Chanel No. 5; she would wear a strand of pearls with a bathing suit (although she also loved swimming naked).

Lorna (who was notoriously unfaithful to Wishart, although she was also devoted to him) had already been involved for several years with the poet Laurie Lee when she first met Lucian during a summer holiday in 1942 with her husband in Southwold, not far from the Freuds' summer cottage in Walberswick. But it was during a 1943 visit to Suffolk to see another lover, David Carr (whom Lucian knew at Cedric Morris's school — he was with Carr when the school burned down), that she and Lucian became an item.

Few men could resist Lorna Wishart, one of seven Garman sisters, three of whom were legendary bohemian beauties; among Kathleen, Lorna, and Mary, their romantic conquests included, in addition to Lucian Freud and Laurie Lee, Vita Sackville West, the composer Ferruccio Busoni, the painter Bernard Meninsky, and the sculptor Jacob Epstein (who would become Freud's father-in-law); Kathleen, the third sister, married Epstein after being his live-in mistress for three decades and bearing his children (including Kitty, Lucian's first wife), despite the fact that at one point his then wife, Margaret, shot her in the shoulder with a pearl-handled pistol.

Lorna, the youngest, was considered the most beautiful of the sisters. She and Lucian made a dazzling couple. As John Craxton told Cressida Connolly, daughter of Cyril Connolly and author of *The Rare and the Beautiful: How the Garman Sisters Captured the Heart of Bohemian London,* "Lucian was a real star turn . . . very, very good-looking, witty, amusing, clever, fun to be with. He was neither English nor German. . . . He was *déraciné,* he wasn't bound by conventions. He was very free. And so was she. Lorna was the most wonderful company, frightfully amusing and ravishingly good-looking; she could turn you to stone with a look. And she had deep qualities, she was not fluttery, she wasn't facile at all. She had a kind of mystery, a mystical inner quality. Any young man would have wanted her." Women agreed. Peggy Guggenheim described her as "the most beautiful creature I had ever seen. She had enormous blue eyes, long lashes, and auburn hair."

Although he was undeniably charismatic and striking, not everyone fell under Lucian's spell. He could appear feral, almost "fox-like," as the photographer John Deakin put it. And, not surprisingly, Lee, his rival for Lorna's affection — at one point they almost came to blows — took a particular dislike to him: " . . . this mad unpleasant youth appeals to a kind of craving she has for corruption." The two spent many late nights in Soho clubs; Richardson spotted them spooning at the Café Caribbean: "I used to see them here, smooching together, always in the dark."

It was Lorna who gave Lucian the stuffed zebra head that figured in one of his first major works, *The Painter's Room* (1943). She had gotten it from the taxidermist Rowland Ward, in Piccadilly, and Freud prized it. According to Feaver, it was his primary possession at Abercorn Place. Lucian brought the exotic head with him when he moved into his own flat in Delamere Terrace, Paddington, later that year. He would remain there for the next three decades.

Freud exulted in the shabby neighborhood, full of lowlifes and criminals, some of whom he came to know (and paint). As Freud himself said of it, "Delamere was extreme and I was conscious of this. A completely unresidential area with violent neighbors," he told Feaver. The seedy atmosphere became a potent element in his work of that time. Writing in the *New Yorker* in 1993, John Richardson described Freud as what might be called a Paddington painter: "Paddington permeates Freud's painting as deeply as Tahiti permeates Gauguin's. Whether or not it manifests itself in Lucian's imagery, the funkiness of the place, as of an unmade bed, and its slightly shabby light, seep into virtually all his work and Londonize it."

Michael Wishart, Lorna's young son (who, in another incident of Bloomsbury-like behavior, later married Anne Dunn, one of Lucian's early lovers), spent many hours in Freud's studio, perhaps first at St. John's Wood, and later in Paddington, posing for Lucian, who drew the then twelve-year-old in many guises, including nude (with an inset of his hand grasping his penis) (*Boy on a Bed,* 1943). He sometimes stayed with Freud, sleeping on the floor at Delamere Terrace. A painter himself, Wishart recalled those days in his memoir *High Diver,* describing a pigeon that Lucian first drew, live, in a portrait of him, then continued to draw, even after the bird died, until its corpse grew moldy and decayed (*Boy with a Pigeon,* 1944).

For all his keen and lifelong love of animals, Freud (like Soutine, whom he admired) reveled in painting them dead, or stuffed, as exemplified in a virtual menagerie of images: *Dead Bird* (1943); *Dead Monkey on a Dish* (1943) (he would do a later version of a dead monkey, in 1950); *Rotted Puffin; Chicken in a Bucket* and *Chicken on a Bamboo Table* (both 1944); *Rabbit on a Chair* (1944); and perhaps his most memorable of this incidental series, the beautiful 1945 *Dead Heron.* He purchased the dead monkeys at Palmer's Pet Stores; the heron was found by Lorna in the marshes. Wishart's daughter by Lee, Yasmin, has called Lorna "Lucian's imagination."

Then there is *The Painter's Room* (1943–44), which features the stuffed zebra head, the most overtly surrealist of Freud's early works, although according to the artist that was not his intention. "I wanted things to look plausible, rather than irrational, if anything eliminating the surrealist look," he said. In it, an oversized zebra head with bright red instead of the standard black stripes, pokes its head through a window and into a room, probably Freud's studio, which contains only a love seat (bought at a junk shop around the corner), a spiky palm tree, a red scarf and a top hat, accoutrements which Feaver calls "the set dressings" of his romance with Wishart. Wishart later bought the painting, for fifty pounds, from Lucian's first solo show at Lefevre gallery in 1944. The zebra also figures in another painting, done at the same time, *Quince on a Blue Table.*

Although he had painted the young girl he met at Coffee An, Lorna, whom he called "Lornie-bird," was the first love interest to serve as Lucian's muse. He did several portraits of her in 1945 that prefigure his later portraits of Kitty, and do not do her considerable beauty justice. Still, they have a certain intensity. "I wanted to convey that she was the first person I was really caught up with," Freud told Gowing. In *Woman with a Tu-*

lip, she sits at a table holding a single flower as red as her smiling lips. In *Woman with a Daffodil,* she is looking down, angry or distraught, and the yellow bloom appears to be wilting.

Lucian was clearly moving into an important new phase of his work, one that was more immediately personal. And, although his paintings were still strongly illustrative, he became more adept with oil paint. According to the critic John Russell, "It was in 1945 that Lucian Freud began to handle oil paint in a specifically adult way. This was due to a new density of involvement with individual human beings. His subject matter had always been autobiographical, in so far as it was related either to objects that he particularly liked ... or to his own immediate surroundings. But he had led until then a life unanchored to specific attachments."

If Lorna had sparked in him a desire for closeness, Freud, who would prove (much like Lorna) to be fundamentally incapable of romantic fidelity, had already begun cheating on her with a new lover, a stunning, young, blonde actress, who was, according to Michael Wishart, "as beautiful as it is possible to be."

When Lorna discovered that he had a new lover, she abandoned him. Freud's exploits following her departure read like pulp fiction. First he followed her to Sussex, where she lived with her family, holing up with Peter Watson. Then he showed up in a cabbage patch, armed with a gun, which he fired, threatening to shoot either her or himself. He also stormed her house, riding bareback on a huge white horse. And, in conciliation, he gave her a tiny white kitten, which she called White Puss.

Although she kept the kitten (and even painted it), Lorna didn't take Freud back. According to Craxton, Lucian never totally got over her. "Lucian was genuinely in love with her, but she never went back to him. It was the great love of his life. He said to me — I've never forgotten — 'I'm never ever going to love a woman more than she loves me,' and I don't think he ever did again. He never really forgot her. He wrote letters saying, 'I still love Lornie and miss her.'" Perhaps symbolically, he abandoned the zebra head in the hall outside his studio.

Lorna was the first of the large-eyed, waif-like beauties that Freud became strongly attached to; the next, Kitty Garman (Lorna's niece), would become his wife. (In a strange coincidence, Lee also married one of Lorna's nieces, Kathy.)

In 1946, not long after Lucian and Lorna broke up, Freud spent an influential two-month interlude in Paris, where he met Picasso and Giacometti. With Watson's financial assistance, he arrived in the City of Light in June and took a room at the Hotel D'Isly, at the corner of Rue Jacob and Rue Bonaparte, which he shared with Michael Wishart. The two would saunter forth every Sunday to the Ile de la Cité, where Freud painted Michael at the Marche aux Oiseau. Even then, he insisted his model remain motionless for hours at a time, as he captured every detail.

It is hard to imagine anyone making much of an impression on Picasso, but Lucian managed this feat, wearing tartan trousers, his old Merchant Navy sweater, and a fez (something he also affected in London). Freud also spent time with — and posed for — Giacometti, who became a role model, and with the poet Olivier Larronde, whom he painted with two parrots. He also socialized with Balthus, Boris Kochko, Christian Bérard — of whom he did a wonderful portrait — and Marie-Laure de Noailles, with whom he traveled to Vienna, so that she could place a plaque on Sigmund's house at Berggasse 19. (According to Richardson, Lucian had not been to Vienna since a visit to his grandfather on the eve of the Anschluss ten years earlier, when he was twelve.) "Lucian appeared to fit so naturally into the postwar, avant-garde, Left Bank life that some of us were afraid dismal Philistine London would lose him. But the very dinginess of England turned out to be more conducive to the practice of art," wrote Richardson of Freud's Paris sojourn.

Lucian would return to Paris three years later, when he

eloped with his second wife, Caroline Blackwood. But before returning to England, he spent several idyllic months with John Craxton in Greece, on the island of Poros, a trip also funded by Watson. The two painters first tried to get to Europe by stowing away on a Breton fishing boat. When that failed, they sailed to the Scilly Isles, where they painted palms, puffins, and the sea. With an advance that Watson got them from the London Gallery, Craxton went on to Athens, while Freud went first to Paris.

In September, Freud joined Craxton, who had arranged rooms on Poros, in Greece, and spent five months there. He and Craxton had a joint show together of their Greek work (as well as later pieces) at the London Gallery in 1947.

The two young painters inspired each other, and Freud filled a sketchbook with drawings of the flora and fauna on the island. Among the paintings he did were a portrait of their landlady's son, *Head of a Greek Man* (1946), which was acquired by Craxton, who admired Freud's "limpid and luminous" style, and a portrait of Craxton, *Portrait of a Man* (1946), as well as *Still Life with Green Lemon* (with a hint of Freud's face peering around the window).

Craxton described a typical day: "I'm off again in a day to an island where lemons and oranges melt in the mouth and goats snatch the last fig leaves off small trees. The corn is yellow and rustles and the sea is harplike on volcanic shores ..." Craxton, like Michael Wishart, complained of the "absolute misery" of posing for Lucian. "He always started with an eyeball, then he imprisoned the eye and then an eyebrow, then a nostril." Presumably when Craxton made his charming pencil portrait of Freud at the time, he was more forgiving.

As Francis Outred, international director of postwar and contemporary art at Christie's, London, observes: "They were very close, thick as thieves. I have seen sketchbooks where you can't tell their drawings apart. Their painting styles were very similar, but after that they diverged both personally and artistically."

Indeed, although they had lived together for almost two years at Abercorn Place, their friendship would later sour. "We lived and painted happily . . . we were inseparable . . . like brothers . . . I learned close scrutiny from Lucian and Lucian learned to draw, plan pictures and understand what can be done with color," Craxton said. But while Craxton valued Freud's work, Freud ultimately dismissed Craxton's after first selling those he owned to pay off his gambling debts. Many years later, when Craxton wanted to sell his Freuds, Lucian supposedly prevented him by writing "Craxton is a cunt" in the margins of the canvases.

Whatever originally caused their later mutual bitterness, it was never resolved. Although Craxton, like many of Freud's close cronies, from Watson to one of his dearest friends, Francis Bacon, was gay, Freud, while he may have been what his grandfather called "polymorphously perverse," was hyperactively heterosexual; by the end of his life he had famously had countless female lovers (many of them much younger than himself) and fathered at least fourteen children, most of them out of wedlock. As the painter Anne Dunn, who had an affair with him in the late 1940s, told Nancy Schoenberger, the author of *Dangerous Muse,* a biography of Lucian's second wife, Caroline Blackwood, "A lot of men and women were in love with Lucian."

4

London Days

B Y NOW FREUD cut a familiar and flamboyant figure in London. He affected an over-the-top bohemian style, attired in a huge overcoat and a fez, often with a hawk strapped to his wrist. According to Joan Wyndham, with whom he had a brief affair after he and Lorna broke up, Freud wore his grandfather Sigmund's dark, fur-collared greatcoat. He kept sparrow hawks as pets, and at one point, a kestrel, which Richardson described as large and vicious, and other observers wrongly identified as "a condor with a six-foot wingspan" or "a falcon, which swoops around the room, and alights on the master's wrist." Freud fed the birds rats that he shot with a Luger along the canal. "I was always excited by birds. If you touch wild birds, it's a marvelous feeling."

Wyndham, a writer, recalled Lucian's idiosyncratic eyes. It was something Carola Zentner also remarked on. "He had this strange sort of tic, of opening his eyes very wide and then screwing them up." Joan described Freud's eyes as constantly darting back-and-forth, hawklike. Or as one journalist said of Freud, "A nervous man, his eyes dart about like fleas in a snuff box." (It is a trait he shared with one of his daughters, Jane McAdam Freud, who does an uncanny imitation of this disturbing tic.)

According to Wyndham, Freud liked to troll in the park for young waifs, whom he would then bring home, as she put it in her book, *Anything Once,* "like stray kittens." She met him in

1946 at a New Year's Eve party given by the poet William Empson, and went back to his studio with him that night, later writing: "In an icy bed I made love to an intriguing mind and a finely chiseled face, but no more."

She described their first encounter in some detail: "I was wondering whether to get sloshed when I noticed a boy watching me from the other side of the room. He was thin and hawklike with hair growing low on his forehead and eyes that darted furtively from side to side. Eventually he came up to me and told me he was called Lucian Freud. After we had talked for a long time he opened a trap door in the floor and took me down some rickety stairs to a nursery. . . . He pushed me back . . . and kissed me." Their host, however, was furious that they were canoodling in his children's room and made them leave.

Back at Lucian's studio, "it was freezing cold, and there was a funny sort of smell. I finally tracked this down to a rather depressed looking hawk who was sitting on the floor of his cage pecking at the remains of a very dead mouse. I have to admit that Lucian made me feel slightly uncomfortable — he was so twitchy, and generated such an intense nervous energy. . . . Next morning Lucian spent hours drawing the hawk, which looked just like him. Every filament on every feather was meticulously recorded — he seemed to be dissecting his subject rather than drawing it."

When they left the studio later that morning, "He opened the hawk's cage and fastened the reluctant bird to his wrist with a thong. . . . Life with Lucian was never easy, as he was so unpredictable . . ." Before long, however, Wyndham realized that she was about to be replaced by "this dark girl with huge eyes . . ." (the girl was Kitty Garman).

However short their affair, Freud made a lasting impression on Wyndham, who described making love to him in an interview with Schoenberger as "like going to bed with a snake." According to her, Freud was "dangerous, not just litigious, you could get fire bombs in your letter box. He has done that. He has done horrible things to people in this town. I am frightened of him." Wyndham herself also dropped a bit of a bomb. "One of his most dangerous things was that he never allowed himself or the women to use contraception. He had an absolute veto. There are children of his all over London. He had children he never even knew about."

Although Freud had fond memories of his grandfather (one of his earliest was of Sigmund amusing him by taking out his dentures and snapping them), in later years he deliberately distanced himself from the famous doctor, insisting that he had read very little of his work, and didn't really admire psychoanalysis. But at the time, according to Wyndham, he made much of the family connection. "He never stopped thinking about him. All the time quoting his grandfather." Certainly, despite deeply rooted British anti-Semitism (which Freud himself encountered), his celebrated lineage could not have hurt him in his quest to mingle with London society.

Wyndham conceded that Lucian was "enormously charming and good-looking," but he was also totally self-absorbed. "He would talk only about himself and his art. In eight months [during which she lived with him], I can't remember him ever asking me one intimate question about myself." He could also be cutting and cruel. He once ran into her on a train, and when she asked to borrow money for the ticket, he said, "No, I couldn't, but I'm sure you'll make it on the train." Wyndham said that when they were lovers Freud explained to her that his relationships with women were ultimately limited because "as soon as I begin to respect or love her, she becomes my mother! I can't make love to her."

It has become almost a cliché to analyze artists and diagnose their various psychopathologies. However, it is interesting to note that Freud exhibited a number of characteristics that have been linked to Asperger's syndrome (or mild autism), a diagnosis that has become so overused that it was recently removed from the *Diagnostic and Statistical Manual of Mental Disorders* (DSM), and instead combined with autism spectrum disorder. In the last few years, a number of general-interest feature articles have reported the exponentially exploding population of people who are diagnosed—or self-diagnosed—with some form of autism—that is, are "on the spectrum."

While it is not necessary—and certainly not diagnostically possible—to give a clinical label to Freud's personality type, it is difficult to ignore a few of the artist's salient idiosyncracies: his acute attention to detail, bordering on obsessive compulsive disorder; his womanizing and gambling; his obvious difficulty relating to people; and his intense love of and ability to relate to animals. Several of his children have recently said they believe it is credible that he had Asperger's (although at least one vehemently disagrees). And a distant relative, Dania Jekel (the great-great-granddaughter of Sigmund Freud, and the head of the Asperger's Association of New England), believes that some of Lucian's traits are consistent with "telltale signs," particularly his strong affinity with animals.

"When you spoke to him, every action was being reflected [or mirrored] . . . your every action is noticed," says his daughter, Jane McAdam. "So you understand that this person isn't like other people, first. Second that you are being noticed in a way that no one will ever notice you again or ever has done before. It's not just hanging on your every word, he's looking at your every movement and reacting to your every expression or emotion. Which is a very, very odd behavioral trait."

As Carola Zentner observes: "His natural speech was not that natural. He was not a natural talker at all. I think he found it quite difficult to chat. His speech was very tortured. If I look back I would say that he found it very difficult to fall into a conventional mode of conversation. He didn't always look at you when he had a conversation. He had his eyes half shut, and only focused on you in kind of snatches."

David McAdam Freud never knew his father during his childhood, and saw him very infrequently as an adult. Still, he told *The Independent* in February 2013, "I think he had Asperger's. I don't think he had the ability to empathize normally with people. I think if you ever met him, Asperger's would have screamed out at you. . . . My dad was famous for the intensity of his gaze, but I think the gaze was his way of coping with [it]."

Asked about his comment to the paper, David explains, "It's speculative on my part. But he looked very intently . . . and I think the effort to look had to do with having to overcome the inability to look at people." In addition, David says, "He just didn't do hugging or like other people to do hugging."

And then there was the addictive nature of his personality. In that respect, Lucian was very much his grandfather's grandson. Consider Sigmund's addictive habits: cigars, cocaine, and for that matter, collecting Egyptian antiquities, which he not only filled his study with, but also frequently brought to the dining table to admire and fondle.

As Peter Gay wrote in his biography of Sigmund Freud, "If Freud's helpless love for cigars attests to the survival of primitive oral needs, his collecting of antiquities reveals residues in adult life of no less primitive anal enjoyments." Freud himself called his "partiality for the prehistoric" "an addiction second in intensity only to his nicotine addiction." His consulting room was stuffed with sculptures "strewn over every available surface."

It's not such a stretch to link Sigmund's particular addictions to Lucian's: women, gambling, and painting. It is impossible to clinically state that Lucian Freud (or Sigmund for that matter) was "on the spectrum," since neither was ever diagnosed with Asperger's (a relatively recent psychiatric term). But Lucian clearly perceived the world differently than others. His extreme process of perception, and of microscopically examining people repeated times in order to produce paintings with an excruciating level of detail, was perhaps not so much an aesthetic choice as an instinctive strategy, a coping mechanism to transmute an inherited behavioral tic into highly original art.

Painting people was Freud's most profound way of relating to them. But even this was a tortured process, requiring multiple sittings, and the intense scrutiny more typical of a laboratory scientist than a painter. "I'm interested, really interested in them as animals and part of liking to work from them naked is that I can see more," Freud said in a BBC interview in December 1991.

When it came to his actual technique of painting, Freud imposed strict inhibitions on himself. "I had certain rules and I suppose those rules were very exclusive. Never putting paint on top of paint. Never touching anything twice. And I didn't want the thing to look arty (which I considered handmade); I wanted them to look as if they came about on their own," he told Feaver.

Anne Dunn described the ordeal of posing for Freud, which she found "mentally painful—because the sitter has to give so much back to Lucian that the sitter in fact feels devoured and digested and regurgitated almost and it also, for myself personally, gave me acute anxiety . . . I didn't feel I had the strength to go on."

Freud never veered from his obsessive scrutiny. But while his early work was graphically driven and based on his well-honed drawing skills, he would, by midcareer, make a seismic leap to a totally different kind of graphic depiction, one in which each hair and wrinkle, while microscopically examined, is no longer flat and linear, but painted with a fugue-like impasto. Yet both his meticulous portraits of the 1940s and his intensely observed 1980s portraits share a characteristic feature; Freud's forensic curiosity gives his depiction of his subjects an aura of taxidermy; they have been mercilessly pinned, like something from Nabokov's butterfly collection, to the canvas. You can almost smell the formaldehyde. It is as if, like his precious zebra head, his various models have been artfully preserved.

"I want paint to work as flesh ... I know my idea of portraiture came from dissatisfaction with portraits that resembled people. I would wish my portraits to be *of* the people, not like them. Not having a look of the sitter, *being* them. I didn't want to just get a likeness like a mimic, but to *portray* them, like an actor. As far as I am concerned the paint *is* the person. I want it to work for me just as flesh does," he told Gowing.

By the mid-1940s, Freud's subject matter became almost exclusively people, often people that he knew, or was intimately involved with. His friend Bruce Bernard observed: "At the heart of Freud's work is the single-figure portrait. The essence of his genius in the perception of human beings is felt most keenly when he has asked one person who interests him, both in look and character, to submit to his scrutiny and help him realize their truest possible image in paint." As Caroline Blackwood wrote in a 1974 catalogue essay, Freud focussed on "Humanity, magnified by the cruel scrutiny of a microscope," although she called his paintings of the '40s and '50s his most "romantic and gentle style."

The best examples of work from this time are Freud's extraordinary portraits of Kitty Garman. Done with a fine sable brush, they resemble the meticulous work of the Flemish school, more than any modern portraiture. In them, the characteristics of Freud's earlier work — the flatness, the extreme attention to detail — are polished to perfection, but something new has crept in, a sense, however remote, of personal connection that goes beyond acute clinical observation.

"Everything is equally there, and must be equally described,"

Robert Hughes wrote of Freud's work of the early '40s. "This objectivity, this evenness of attention, mingled with a barely veiled anxiety about the otherness of all objects — rooms, face, plants, furniture — lies at the core of Freud's early work."

But in his memorable images of Kitty, Freud manages to imbue his precisely realized graphic style with an essence of emotional substance. While one could hardly say the paintings breathe, their subject has feelings — and those feelings are transmitted — both to the artist and by him: transference — as his grandfather identified it — manifested in paint.

As Robert Hughes later wrote about Freud's *Girl with Roses* (in which Kitty was newly pregnant with their first child): "It is masterly in the smoothness of its transitions, from the detail of hair (in which every strand seems to be in place ...) to the finely modulated flatness of the flesh.... Everything is equally scrutinized, the broken caning of the chair ... no less than the rose petals and the miniscule structure of reflections in those huge, tawny, apprehensive eyes. What other modernist portrait ... has deployed such a consideration of detail amassed and refined to so haunting an erotic tenderness?" Indeed, Freud's early, pristine style caused Herbert Read to later famously label him "the Ingres of Existentialism."

The artist met the model who inspired this "masterpiece of Lucian Freud's twenties" at the Café Royale, in 1946. He was introduced to her by Lorna Wishart. According to their first child, Annie, "Lorna planned it. She got tired of him and passed him along. It was Lorna's doing."

As one of the mythical Garmans, Kitty already had a sterling bohemian birthright, which was only enhanced by the fact that her father was Jacob Epstein. Although it was to be a troubled marriage, she seemed to fit Freud's romantic and erotic type to a T: very girlish, with immense, expressive eyes. Freud beautifully captured those eyes from the earliest drawing he made of her, before they were married, the lovely *Head of a Girl* (1947), through the last portrait he made of her, the pensive *Girl with a White Dog* (1951–52).

Kitty Garman, née Kathleen Eleonora Garman, was born on August 27, 1926, to Kathleen Garman and Jacob Epstein, the second of four children the couple would have before they married in 1956. Kitty was not brought up by her mother — whose lifestyle, living in a stark, unheated Bloomsbury studio as Epstein's mistress — was not considered appropriate. Instead, she was brought up by her grandmother, Margaret, in Herefordshire. She had artistic ambitions, and was studying art at the Central School of Arts and Crafts in London, with Bernard Meninsky, at the time she met Lucian. A great beauty with a "nervous disposition," she was, like Lucian, highly observant and original, although she tended to be self-effacing. Her daughter, Annie, later described her as a rarified "woman of accoutrements, narrow-ankled, wearing fine calf-skin, and smelling of lemon-scented cologne."

As the illegitimate daughter of Jacob and Kathleen, Kitty was familiar with the bohemian lifestyle, even if she didn't really become a part of it until her late teens, when she moved to London and lived with her mother. She had sat for her father many times, and she considered her wildly unconventional aunts, Lorna and Ruth, to be role models. She was not easily shocked. Although her mother had been shot by Epstein's enraged wife, Margaret, several years before she was born, it was a tale she often told. Lucian's intense and unconventional artistic persona was recognizable territory. The two got married in 1948, about a year after they met. They were a ready-made beautiful couple.

As Annie describes her parents' relationship: "I think they were terribly impressed with each other. In earlier times than ours, to be as good-looking as they were as a couple was a very huge thing. They were known. They dressed to set each other off, to look amazing together, you know dazzling. They introduced one another to unheard of things. For example, my father came from a family where for generations, they were not in any sense religious Jews. The idea of a spiritual life and all that sort of thing was not really existent. I think my father found the sort of Englishness of my mother, her lineage really, really interesting. And for my mother, to be the wife of an amazing artist, doing things that absolutely nobody else was doing, was damned exciting, and the glamour and the foreignness of Jewishness. [Even though Kitty had a Jewish father, she had been brought up Catholic by her grandmother.] You know how a couple can love the fact that they are a couple and celebrate how they look together and the mystique that surrounds them as a pair, and the way they complement and supplement each other and underlines their characters."

Freud made a number of stunning portraits of Kitty, including *Girl in a Dark Jacket* and *Girl with a Kitten* (both 1947) and *Girl with Leaves* (1948), constituting a painted record of their courtship and marriage. In them, particularly *Girl with a Kitten* (a play on her name), in which Kitty, looking menaced, is oddly clutching the kitten by the throat, the most striking feature is the apprehensive fear in her eyes, a look which is finally replaced by sadness, or resignation, in *Girl with a White Dog*. "The viewer would be hard put to say whether the woman or the dog is painted more lovingly," wrote one journalist. (The bull terrier was one of a pair that had been given to the couple as a wedding present.) There is only one loosely drawn sketch, *Mother and Baby* (1949), in which Kitty is smiling.

But marriage and fatherhood had not altered Freud's philandering ways — or for that matter, Kitty's. Just a month after she gave birth to their first child, Annie, in 1948, Freud left for Connemara, Ireland, where he had a three-week tryst with Anne Dunn at the Zetland Hotel. Several haunting works remain from this trip: a drawing of a boat, *Boat, Connemara* (1948), which sold for $550,000 at auction in February 2012, and two of Anne, including a pastel, *Interior Scene*. The Christie's catalogue describes this "mysterious" piece: "A small woman stands partially obscured in the dusky shadows. It is his paramour Anne Dunn, here standing in a bedroom at the Zetland Hotel, her brilliant blue eyes framed by parted curtain drapes." Prominent in the atmospheric painting (reminiscent of *Hotel Bedroom,* a portrait Lucian later did of his second wife, Caroline Blackwood) is a spiky, thorned plant, suggestive of the difficult situation. (Ironically, in later years Kitty became friendly with the Howell family, who owned *Boat, Connemara,* and would, wittingly or unwittingly, sit beneath it when visiting them.)

According to Francis Outred, "The picture of Anne Dunn is one of the great masterpieces of his work, and it's because of the faith of representation and detail, as much as the subject. It's a very interesting depiction because she is hiding behind the curtain, as well she should be. There is a double meaning in the image, and I think he's purposefully done that, making a comment on what he was doing. It is as much about the artist himself as the subject, and Freud wants to put himself in that position."

To Anne Dunn, Freud seemed "to have much more life than anyone else I'd ever seen. He seemed so electric." Although Lucian at first missed his train to Connemara, Dunn described their ensuing Irish interlude as "quite domestic. I wanted to please him. I think it was as simple as that." But when it ended, she was bitter. "The actual fact of being used by Lucian, with whom I was having a very close relationship, it does mean that the fact of the painting takes on another meaning. With other painters that I sat for, I felt more like a still life, like an apple or bottle or something. But it didn't mean that at the end, the bottle or the apple would be thrown out. I had a very strong relationship with Lucian, and I loved him very much and it was like being flung out of the Garden of Eden."

By the time Lucian painted *Girl with a White Dog*, the marriage was clearly in trouble, although it would take another year to completely unravel. In 1952, Kitty asked for a divorce from Freud. As Annie has said of Lucian's Kitty portraits, "My mother was, as you can see in the paintings, a great beauty, and she was immensely proud to know that *Girl with a White Dog* is Tate Britain's biggest-selling postcard. I think the effect of sitting for him in their short and not always very happy marriage did tell on her, but I know that she looked back with pride at her beauty being so celebrated."

As Gowing wrote of the series, "Love is the condition of being at one another's mercy. The girl's capacity for suffering must serve for both; we guess this couple works it overtime. The remorseless sharpness of the focus on her eyes reveals them, each time in a new dimension, minutely displaced. They are perpetually watchful for an emergency that is inevitable."

Still, says Annie, infidelity is not what ultimately caused the marriage to fail. "My father was spectacularly unfaithful. My mother was pretty unfaithful, too. But although unfaithfulness had a part in destroying their marriage, it really involved my father's aspirations to want to be with the top echelons of society that my mother found intolerable, especially when she herself was suffering financially."

According to Annie, Lucian had a "violently closely held belief to carry on with lords and ladies." After both had remarried (Kitty happily in 1955 to the economist Wynne Godley, a breathtakingly handsome man who served as the model for her father's sculpture, *Saint Michael Spearing the Devil* at Coventry Cathedral) there would be a bitter court battle over Lucian including both their daughters, Annie as well as Annabel (born in 1952), in a "very, very grand social life, and staying at the Ritz in Paris, and hobnobbing with Lady Diana Cooper."

Even more abhorrent to Kitty and Wynne was Freud's relationship with the Viscount and Viscountess Lambton, whom

Annie describes as "a glamorous couple, fabulously wealthy. There were lots of bizarre myths and legends about them. They were called the 'unlucky Lambtons' because of various terrible disasters." Freud, who·painted "Bindy" Lambton, also had a long-term affair with her. "I was very, very close to Bindy Lambton and to one of her elder daughters. My mother and stepfather did not like this development," says Annie.

Freud would have ample opportunity to rub shoulders with aristocracy — and even royalty — in his next romantic relationship, which had begun while he was still married to Kitty, with Lady Caroline Blackwood.

5

Beautiful People

L UCIAN FREUD WAS already mingling with high society — quite literally — when he first set eyes on Caroline Blackwood. It was at her coming out party in 1949,
which, as she recalled years later, took place in a tent on the
banks of the Thames (although other accounts say it was at
Londonderry House). "I barely remember it," she told *Town and
Country* magazine in 1993. "Somebody brought Lucian Freud
and he created a stir by falling over Princess Margaret. He was
steadying himself on the back of her sofa — he was drunk — and
then he just tipped over and went onto her. She was outraged
because she had no sense of humor. Her mother was there —
the Queen, now the Queen Mother — and was amused." (Freud
would paint her daughter, Queen Elizabeth, in 2001.)

Not long afterwards, Lucian was involved in another dramatic incident involving Princess Margaret at a ball, this time
one thrown by Lady Rothermere, a.k.a. Ann Fleming, Ian Fleming's wife. He and Francis Bacon had arrived late at the grand
gathering, just in time to catch Princess Margaret singing Cole
Porter — not very well. Much to everyone's horror, some vocal
booing ensued during her rendition of "Let's Do It."

The boos came from Bacon, a close friend whom Freud had
first met through the painter Graham Sutherland in 1945. It was
a pivotal relationship, and Bacon would have a major influence
on Freud, before a final falling out several decades later. Freud

remembered the Princess Margaret story differently, telling Martin Gayford that it was he who had brought Bacon to Warwick House, Lady Rothermere's home, and that Princess Margaret ("the most marvelous, glamorous person at that time") was accompanied by Noel Coward on the piano, before she was interrupted by Bacon's heckling. Freud was forced to take the blame.

Freud had first become friendly with Ann Fleming in the late 1940s, when she was married to Esmond Rothermere, and he remained friends with her after her marriage to Ian Fleming in 1952. He even went to stay with them soon after their marriage, at Goldeneye, their villa in Jamaica, while Fleming was writing the first Bond book, *Casino Royale.* Freud took a banana boat to get there, and did an anxious-looking self-portrait (1952).

Ann was a renowned hostess, famous for gathering the crème de la crème of the political, literary, and bohemian set, and Freud had become one of her protégés. She was also a surrogate mother to a stunningly beautiful young woman named Caroline Blackwood, and had helped her get a job at the *Picture Post.*

It's not quite clear from various accounts if Lucian first actually met Caroline that night (as Caroline told the *New York Times* critic Michael Kimmelman) or at another of Ann's evenings, but there was an instant mutual attraction. Caroline claimed that he immediately asked to do her portrait. "I think Lucian knows exactly who he wants to paint—I mean, across the room."

"He was attractive, intelligent, and different from anyone else she had met," wrote Caroline's daughter, Ivana Lowell, of Lucian's appeal for her mother. "He also had all the qualities that she knew would most horrify her mother. Lucian was still married. He was impoverished. And he was Jewish. He was absolutely unsuitable in every way, and therefore he couldn't have been more perfect." As Blackwood herself recalled him, "Lucian was fantastic, very brilliant, incredibly beautiful, though not in a movie-star way. I remember he was very mannered, he wore those long side whiskers, which nobody else had then. And he wore funny trousers, deliberately. He wanted to stand out in a crowd, and he did."

Ann Fleming encouraged the match. Lucian would drop by the *Picture Post* offices to pursue Caroline, and things soon got serious. "Lucian began to come round the office to visit me — he was beginning to be very interested. He was about ten years older than me, and separated from his first wife, Kitty ... Lucian was beautiful, Byronic, with his shock of dark hair and his aquiline face, and he made everything we did exciting, even if it was just buying the newspaper," she recalled.

By 1951, they were seriously involved, even though Freud was still married to Kitty, with whom he briefly traveled to Dublin in September. Kitty wrote to her mother that they kept moving from boarding house to hotel, and that Dublin was "like nowhere else, very human and sad and lost." That same year Freud won the Arts Council of Great Britain Prize (500 pounds) for his painting, *Interior in Paddington,* an enigmatic double-portrait of sorts, which gives equal billing to his friend and neighbor, Harry Diamond, and a familiar spiky palm tree.

Caroline was to become the second great love of his life. Born on July 16, 1931, she was nine years younger than Lucian. When they met, she was eighteen and he was twenty-six. Besides being brainy and beautiful, with the requisite waif-like slenderness and huge eyes, Lady Caroline Hamilton Temple Blackwood was heiress to the Guinness ale fortune. She was the daughter of Lord and Lady Dufferin. Her father, Lord Dufferin, was Basil Hamilton-Temple-Blackwood, the fourth Marquess of Dufferin and Ava, and her mother, Maureen, was a fabled "glorious Guinness girl," who after her marriage to Blackwood became the Marchioness of Dufferin and Ava. Her great-grandfather, at one point the viceroy of India, was rumored to be the illegitimate son of Disraeli, something Caroline delighted in. Her father died when she was thirteen, and her mother left the rearing of Caroline and her sisters to a succession of nannies.

Caroline grew up in Clandeboye, the ancient Blackwood family manse in Bangor, Northern Ireland, decorated with a stuffed rhinoceros head and various Egyptian artifacts, including a mummified hand and the ropes used to lower mummies into their tombs. The place even had a "folly," a tower built in honor of Caroline's great-great grandmother, Helen, in 1861, engraved with lines written to her by famous poets, including Tennyson. (In her biography of Blackwood, *Dangerous Muse,* Nancy Schoenberger makes her family background sound like something out of Edgar Allan Poe.)

It wasn't just the Blackwood-Guinness family wealth that was a magnet to Freud, but the fabulous social imprimatur. Her father Basil had been a good friend of Evelyn Waugh's, and a member of the "Brideshead Revisited" group. As his daughter Annie pointed out, Lucian Freud at the time was a driven social climber, not an easy feat for a starving artist who was also a German-Jewish émigré in London. Although Freud told Gayford that he had "not often experienced" anti-Semitism, he encountered it with frequency during his pursuit of — and eventual marriage to — Caroline.

Waugh, for one, took an intense dislike to Freud, writing on several occasions to Nancy Mitford to complain about him. "Yes, I don't like Freud. I knew him before he got into society and didn't like him then. . . . He brings Princess Margaret to nightclubs in saffron socks." After Lucian and Caroline were married, he wrote to Mitford, "You know that poor Maureen's daughter made a runaway match with a terrible Yid?"

Sometimes Freud was insulted to his face. As Caroline recalled it, "One night I took him to a cocktail party my mother was giving in her over-decorated boule house in Sloane Street, and I can tell you, she wasn't pleased. Randolph Churchill was there and he said, in stentorian tones, 'What the bloody hell is Maureen doing, turning her house into a bloody synagogue.' I pretended I hadn't heard, and Lucian pretended *he* hadn't heard, and then the next time Lucian met Randolph somewhere, he knocked him flat on his back, which was rather satisfying." (Lucian had never given up his boyhood habit of punching out his opponents; according to Blackwood, "Lucian anyway was terribly aggressive — he tended to knock down anyone in a bar.")

Lucian's talent, looks, and lineage did not impress Maureen. According to Caroline's sister, Perdita, "She didn't like him because he was really Bohemian looking. . . . He had a shirt open and no tie . . . and so Mother used to get mad at him." At one point, he was invited to a pheasant shoot by Ann Fleming's son, Raymond O'Neill, along with Lord and Lady Dufferin. As Ann wrote of Lucian's "curious holiday" in Ulster, "he was in pursuit of Lady Caroline and was socially a disaster . . . and of course I was blamed for encouraging bizarre tartan-trousered eccentric artists to pursue virginal Marchionesses' daughters." After shocking the guests, according to Fleming, with the speed with which he retrieved pheasants, he further scandalized them when he was discovered having sex with Caroline "on the hearth, beneath dimmed lamps . . ."

It wasn't long before Caroline moved into Freud's Paddington studio. In 1952, the couple eloped to Paris. (They were later legally married in a civil ceremony at the Chelsea Registry Office in London on December 9, 1953.) In Paris, they took up residence in the Hotel La Louisiane, where they lived for about a year. It is there that Freud would paint several portraits of her that would become among his most famous works, particularly *Girl in Bed* (1952) and *Hotel Bedroom* (1954).

But Caroline's exquisite beauty — Ned Rorem, who met her in Paris, said she was one of the most beautiful women he had ever encountered — while it inspired Freud, apparently didn't sate his curiosity or libido. "Even on our honeymoon. We would be sitting in some outdoor café, and every time an even remotely pretty girl walked past, his head would turn and follow her with the most ghastly lascivious eyes," Caroline later told her daughter, Ivana. One friend who went to Paris for their "honeymoon" said it wasn't just his eye that wandered: Freud actually disappeared for a few days.

Their life in Paris was also made difficult by the fact that Caroline's mother, Maureen, angered by her daughter's relationship and scandalous elopement with Freud, which had denied her the pleasure of not only a proper society wedding but a public announcement (that came a year later, when they wed in London), had cut off her allowance, at least temporarily. (Maureen later denied this was the case.) According to Barbara Skelton, then married to Cyril Connolly, during Christmastime 1952, Maureen was still so set against Lucian that he was excluded from a party she was giving. She made a point of never seeing Lucian again during the marriage, and soon after he and Caroline were divorced she ran into Freud at a nightclub and hit him in the face with her purse.

As Caroline recalled, "We lived in Paris almost penniless, but in those days you could live really well there on practically nothing. We stayed in a hotel on the Left Bank, on the Rue de Seine. Lucian was totally absorbed in trying to get his work done and I was totally absorbed in sitting for him."

Still, the couple made the most of their time, socializing with, among others, Marie-Laure de Noailles and Picasso, who painted Caroline's fingernails, an incident that both Caroline and Lucian took pride in recounting years later. As Caroline told Kimmelman, on a visit to the artist's studio, "Picasso asked me if I wanted to see his doves: he had this spiral staircase leading to the roof, and off we go, winding round and round to the top, until we reached these doves in cages, and all around us was the best view of Paris, the best. Whereupon, immediately, standing on this tiny, tiny space, way above the city, Picasso does a complete plunge at me. All I felt was fear. I kept saying, 'Go down the stairs . . .' He said, 'No, No, we are together above the roofs of Paris.' It was so absurd, and to me Picasso was just as old as the hills, an old letch, genius or no."

Somewhere in the midst of "this terrible pass," Picasso found time to paint tiny images on Caroline's fingernails. (As her daughter puts it, "For a while she had her very own Picassos on her nails.") Lucian recalled the anecdote for Martin Gayford while painting his portrait, a year-plus venture that Gayford memorably records in *Man with a Blue Scarf.* "Picasso behaved like a marvelous conjurer. When you left his apartment, you instinctively looked back up at the windows, high above. He was aware of that reflex, because one day when we glanced up like that he was at the window, making bird shapes. . . . When I took Caroline there he painted her fingernails — which were tiny, in any case, because she bit them — with little faces and sun shapes. She kept them for as long as possible, but eventually they disappeared. She was in the flat alone with him for about half an hour. When I asked afterward what had happened, she said, 'I can never, ever tell you.' So I never, ever asked." Lucian went on to observe, "He was very malevolent, absolutely poisonous, not that I minded it much. I asked him once what he liked about a friend we had in common. He replied: 'That I can make her cry whenever I want to.'"

Lucian later got a call from one of Picasso's lovers asking to have her portrait painted; but Lucian said he was otherwise engaged, painting a picture of his wife, the lovely *Girl in Bed* (1952), the first of a quartet of memorable Parisian paintings of Caroline, done just a few months before they were married. In it, a beautiful blonde young woman (it's interesting that, like Kitty in her portraits, she is labeled "girl" in the painting's title) is lying among crumpled white bed linens, leaning on her elbow, her head propped on her hand. Caroline, like the Kitty of Freud's previous connubial portraits, is pensive. But unlike

Freud's palette for Kitty, characterized by the dead pallor of her ivory skin, Caroline's face radiates a warm, golden glow.

Still, it turns out she wasn't so much basking in Freud's attentive gaze (or reflecting on it) as a bit bored. Caroline told her daughter that although she looks wistful in the pictures, actually she was stultified by the process of posing for hours on end, reading Dostoyevsky (*The Idiot* during *Girl in Bed*) and Henry James (*The Tragic Muse* during *Girl Reading*) aloud to Lucian for relief. "Critics said he paints the anguish of our age — but he really paints the anguish of his sitter," she later said. Anguish or not, Robert Hughes pronounced the painting a "masterpiece of Lucian Freud's twenties." It is also palpably tender, something one does not usually associate with Freud's work.

(Many years later, *Girl in Bed* would play a tragic role in a postscript to Caroline's third marriage. In 1977, the poet Robert Lowell, whom Caroline, by then herself a published reporter and novelist, had married five years earlier, died of a heart attack on his way home in a New York taxi, shortly after leaving Caroline in Ireland. He was found dead, clutching the painting; Caroline was later told by Elizabeth Hardwick — his wife just before Caroline — that the hospital had to break his arms to retrieve it.)

Lucian's roving eye and compulsive gambling combined to take a toll, and according to Ivana Lowell's account, the couple frequently quarreled during their prolonged stay at the Hotel La Louisiane. At one point "Lucian pushed my mother out of the hotel room into the corridor and locked the door. She was completely naked, but he refused to let her back in," Ivana wrote in her memoir.

The couple managed to survive together a year or so at the hotel. During their Paris stay, Freud also painted *Girl Reading* (1952) which, desperate for money to pay the hotel bill, Caroline convinced Cyril Connolly to buy, and the luminous *Girl with Starfish Necklace* (1952), in which Caroline, at the time twenty-one, looks barely past adolescence. (It's interesting to note that although in several of the four paintings Lucian made of Caroline in Paris she is lying in bed, in none of them is her body shown, nude or otherwise.)

At this point, Freud had begun to move away from his former emphatically flat style; his portraits were now more three-dimensional, the faces and limbs modeled (and mottled) in a more life-like way; the canvases became less about drawing — or illustrating — and more about really employing paint. The contrast between Freud's treatment of Kitty and that of Caroline is striking; side-by-side you would scarcely know that these portraits were done by the same artist. "The idea of doing paintings where you're conscious of the drawing and not the paint just irritated me, so I stopped doing drawing for many, many years," Freud later said.

When Caroline and Lucian returned to London, they took up residence in Soho, on Dean Street, "in a very pretty kind of prostitute's house," according to Caroline, and quickly became part of its bohemian scene, which included, among other regulars, Francis Bacon, Frank Auerbach, John Deakin, John Minton, and Cyril Connolly. (Meanwhile, Connolly fell in love with not just the painting of Caroline but the woman; at one point Freud had to physically drive him away by kicking him.)

They also bought "a little stone house in Dorset, in real Hardy country. Lucian immediately got a horse.... In Dorset he rode bareback, like a cowboy," Caroline said. According to Michael Wishart, who visited them there, it was a former priory, "a beautiful old building beside a large black lake. Lucian kept horses and bought a lot of marble furniture and painted part of a floral mural on a wall of their dining-room." Wishart was also a frequent breakfast guest in Soho, keeping Caroline company at the "Georgian house" on Dean Street, "as Lucian went to his studio in Paddington as soon as it was light."

Soho social life in the bohemian set centered around three

favorite places: Wheeler's, a classic oyster bar and fish house; the Gargoyle, for the wild, wee hours; and the mythic Colony Room, which was conveniently located on Dean Street. Established by the legendary Muriel Belcher in 1948, it was a small, shabby second-floor room made famous by its hard-boiled, irreverent hostess—and her illustrious clients. "It is not like other clubs at all, more like a cocktail party," observed Paul Potts, a regular. Or as Bacon told Daniel Farson, who chronicled the scene in several books (including *Sacred Monsters*), "It's a place where you can lose your inhibitions. It's different from anywhere else. After all, that's what we all want, isn't it? A place to go where one feels free and easy."

Bacon, Lucian Freud, Frank Auerbach, Michael Andrews, and Tim Behrens gathered there regularly, and collectively they soon became known as "Muriel's Boys" or the "Colony Room Mob." They were also eventually grouped together under the art-historical label "the School of London," which included the painter R. B. Kitaj; it was Kitaj who came up with the name, referring to a British figurative style at odds with the abstract expressionism that was dominating the American art scene at the time, epitomized by the work of de Kooning and Rothko.

The place was later immortalized in a group portrait, *The Colony Room*, painted by Michael Andrews, in which a very recognizable Freud is more or less the central figure, although in reality Bacon (whose back is shown) was probably its most regular habitué. The two artists would hole up in a corner, chatting, "Mr. Freud reserved, ironic, abstemious (and conspicuously heterosexual) . . . Bacon more expansive, especially while the drink flowed," recalled Geoffrey Wheatcroft in an homage to Belcher, "the greatest of the Soho hostesses."

According to Farson, Lucian went to the Colony Room mainly to see Francis, and would depart early in the evening so he could put in a full night at the studio. "I remember Lucian sidling into the seedy room with a swift glance of recognition as he saw Muriel, followed by a furtive sidelong appraisal as his eyes raked the present company to see if there was anyone worth talking to. When the company pleased him, there were few sharper conversationalists. He would shatter my naivete as he turned accepted theories upside down, his wit enhanced by the slight, lingering German accent which gave an added emphasis to every word." Freud and Bacon would together, along with Ben Nicholson, represent Britain at the 1954 Venice Biennale (Lucian with, among other works, *Hotel Bedroom*).

Over time, Freud painted portraits of a number of Colony Room fixtures: a prophetic, doomed-looking painting of the artist John Minton (1952), who killed himself five years later; the sardonic photographer John Deakin (1963–64); as well as Michael Andrews, Timothy Behrens (*Red-Haired Man on a Chair*, 1962–63) and Frank Auerbach (1975–76).

Caroline called the self-perpetuating social cycle "a whole kind of Soho life. Going out to Wheeler's, and then the Colony [which closed early, at 11 p.m.] and the Gargoyle, was the thing with that crowd."

The Gargoyle, with its shabby-chic mirrored ballroom (originally designed by Matisse but later renovated), was the last stop. As Andrew Sinclair wrote in his 1993 biography of Bacon, "The Gargoyle housed the residue of post-war Bohemia, where the aristocrats and the artists, the privileged and the patronized, would meet and drop the barriers of class, particularly if their homosexuality forced them into a clandestine security at a place that did not consider their preferences to be criminal acts." According to Sinclair, one night Bacon and Freud got into a scuffle with the editor of the *Spectator*, whose "rough trade" boys tousled with the artists; Freud jumped on the back of one while Bacon kicked the other. A lawsuit was threatened but none ensued. Another time, Jean-Paul Sartre and Simone de Beauvoir were there, and both remarked on Lucian's striking looks, Sartre asking who "the good-looking one" was, and de Beauvoir calling him the only man there "attractive enough to go home with."

Much of the time, it was filled with the bright and beautiful of all sexual persuasions, usually somewhat soused. (Apparently Lucian didn't drink much, unlike Caroline, who became an alcoholic.) As Caroline described the Gargoyle, "You would wander in any night and find the cleverest people in England." These included Graham Greene, Cyril Connolly, Peter Watson, Dylan Thomas, John Deakin, George Weidenfeld, Stephen Spender, Lady Diana Cooper, not to mention Lucian's old love, Lorna Wishart, as well her son, Michael, and his wife, Anne Dunn, who had met through Bacon. Among the most bright and beautiful were Caroline and Lucian themselves.

6

Letting Go

AS IMPORTANT IN many ways as either of his marriages (and longer lasting), Freud's relationship with Francis Bacon flourished in the early 1950s. Freud called him the wildest and wisest man he had ever met, and they were for several decades the best of friends. Michael Peppiatt, one of Bacon's biographers, wrote of their strong affinity:

> Like Bacon, Freud had an endless curiosity about other people and the human comedy in general: the two artists had no problem in abandoning a discussion about poetry — of which they were both perceptive readers — to regale each other with choice bits of gossip about their friends and acquaintances; as obsessive gamblers, they could also compare notes on how they had fared at the various gaming tables they both frequented. Both painters also had tumultuous private lives and since for a very long time they met on an almost daily basis they tended to be drawn in to each other's latest escapades or indeed emotional crises.

Bacon's influence would ultimately push Freud's painting into a pivotal new dimension, from flat and linear to fully fleshed out. Freud first met Bacon in 1945, when he asked another friend, the painter Graham Sutherland, whom he thought was the best painter in England. Sutherland instantly responded, "Oh, someone you've never heard of, he's like a cross

between Vuillard and Picasso." Sutherland invited both Freud
and Bacon to spend a weekend in Kent; they met for the trip at
Victoria Station. "Once I met him, I saw him a lot," Freud told
Feaver.

That's an understatement. As Caroline Blackwood put it, "I
had dinner with him [Bacon] nearly every night for more or less
the whole of my marriage to Lucian. We also had lunch" (most
likely at Wheeler's, Bacon's favorite restaurant). Observed Anne
Dunn, who along with her husband Michael Wishart spent a
great deal of time with Lucian, Caroline, and Bacon at various
Soho haunts, "Lucian had a kind of hero-worshipping crush on
Bacon, although I don't think it was ever consummated."

Freud was attracted not only to Bacon's talent but to his
edge; risk taking and a scorn of all convention was something
they shared. Another bond was the addictive nature of their
personalities. While Bacon's drugs of choice were alcohol (particularly champagne), his (often very rough) male lovers, and
gambling, Lucian's addictions were womanizing, gambling, and
painting. (Bacon compared his carousing with Freud's womanizing, saying "To bed, or rather to sleep at three, then up again
at seven, she posing as his model.")

Ironically, Freud claimed to have learned a certain level of
civility from the famously flamboyant Bacon. As he later told
art critic Sebastian Smee, from the start he considered his friend
"*really* admirable. I'll give you a simple example. I used to have
a lot of fights. It wasn't because I liked fighting, it was really
just that people said things to me to which I felt the only reply was to hit them. If Francis was there, he'd say, 'Don't you
think you ought to try to charm them?' And I thought, '*Well*'
. . . before that I never really thought about my behavior, I just
thought about what I wanted to do, and I did it. And quite often I wanted to hit people . . ."

Like Freud, Bacon worked in his studio every day (even after a typically long night), although he did not put in Lucian's

notorious nocturnal hours; but his practice was diametrically different. Although in the 1950s he occasionally used sitters, Bacon worked straight from photographs and reference materials rather than live models, and his technique was intuitive and impetuous, rather than obsessively focused. While Freud's art was based on his skill as a draughtsman, drawing never played a serious part in Bacon's oeuvre.

"His best paintings were done so entirely by inspiration that there is almost no basis of drawing," Freud later said of his former friend. As Sinclair summarized it, Freud built up his images by meticulous detail, while Bacon charged at his subjects in a whirl of brushes, calling the astonishing results creative "accidents." (If at the time Freud was painting in two dimensions, Bacon had found a fourth.)

Freud would visit Bacon's studio nearly every afternoon. As he described it, "He had this wonderful studio, which had been [John Everett] Millais'" and was paid for by one of Bacon's lovers, a "high-powered businessman.... The man was married with children." Freud was struck by how quickly Bacon worked. "Sometimes I'd go round in the afternoon and he'd say, 'I've done something really extraordinary today.' And he'd done it all in that day. Amazing."

Freud and Bacon made portraits of each other; their methods and results a study in contrasts. In fact, Bacon's portrait of Freud, done in 1951, was his first named portrait: "Lucian told me that after Francis asked to paint him, he went round to his studio for the sitting and found that Francis had finished the painting. Which, of course, is the opposite of how Lucian works," recalled Caroline. Indeed, Lucian never sat at all: Bacon had used a photograph of Franz Kafka as a reference. "It isn't very good, but it's lively," Freud later remarked.

Typically, Freud's portrait of Bacon took much longer. For two or three months, in 1952, Freud and Bacon sat "knee to knee," as Freud told Feaver. "He grumbled a bit but sat well and

consistently." The small, exquisite, oil-on-copper painting of
Bacon was spot-on, capturing him unguarded, his gaze downward. "Freud's achievement, at 30, convinced everyone but himself," wrote Gowing. "The Bacon portrait, hanging at the Tate,
quite unobtrusive yet biting like a little serpent when it caught
you, exerted the transfixing spell of an image that is tantamount
to the thing itself." Originally meant to be hung at Wheeler's,
then purchased by the Tate, it was stolen in 1988 while on loan
in Berlin and never recovered. Bacon said it was taken because it
was so good: "The thieves knew exactly what they were doing."

Bacon would go on to do dozens of portraits of Freud over
the years, among them a double-portrait of Lucian and their
mutual friend Frank Auerbach, lolling on a divan without trousers (1964); a portrait of Freud with Bacon's lover George Dyer
(1967); and a triptych, *Three Studies for a Portrait of Lucian
Freud* (1964), that sold for just over $35 million pounds at
Sotheby's in January 2011. An historic record was set in November 2013 when *Three Studies of Lucian Freud* (1969) went
for $142,405,000 at Christie's — the most expensive work of art
ever sold at auction. It was at Bacon's suggestion — "I think you
ought to use these" — that Freud did a sly drawing of his friend,
his undone pants sliding down his hips, at Clifton Hill in 1952.

Thirteen years Freud's senior, Bacon was already beginning
to work in the style that would make him famous by the time
they met, starting with his *Three Studies for Figures at the Base
of a Crucifixion* in 1944. Bacon boldly deconstructed the human
face and form as deliberately as any Cubist. His vision was totally original: portrait as poltergeist. Long before morphing became a routine cinematic special effect, Bacon was wrenching,
wringing, and warping the figures of his subjects as if they were
taffy. His "Screaming Pope" series conveys nearly the same exis-
tential dread as Edvard Munch's *The Scream*. In fact, the primal
scream was a favorite Bacon trope.

Bacon filtered his visceral, Goya-esque visions through images appropriated from movies and the media, years before Warhol would take such source material in a very different direction. X-rays were another major influence on his spectral, ectoplasmic forms. His unique, molten, whirling-dervish images could not have been further from Freud's studied realism. He prized the unique effects of chance, "the slip of the painting hand, the dribble of paint, the collision of shapes," writes Peppiatt. Bacon worked from his fervid imagination; Freud from life.

The two had a major intellectual and artistic impact on each other. But it was Bacon who sparked an aesthetic epiphany in Freud. As Freud put it, "I realized that his work related immediately to how he felt about life. Mine on the other hand seemed very labored.... It was his attitude that I admired. The way he was completely ruthless about his own work." As he told Feaver, "I realized that by working the way I did I couldn't really evolve. The change wasn't perhaps more than one of focus, but it did make it possible for me to approach the whole thing in another way."

Freud and Bacon were bound as much by their art as by their compulsive gambling: risk ruled. Bacon was a notorious gambling addict: he bragged of spending sixteen hours in a casino in Monte Carlo. As he told David Sylvester, "I feel I want to win, but then I feel exactly the same thing in painting. I feel I want to win even if I always lose." (A regular at the Monte Carlo roulette tables, he also often won, once using his loot to rent a villa and party with friends for over a week.) "Nothing is more wonderful and refreshing than being completely cleaned out," he told his sometime gambling companion, Michael Wishart: "Losing is better than winning."

Freud's remarks on the topic are similar. He claimed to have started gambling as a child in funfairs, and really became hooked in 1944, he said in an interview with Sebastian Smee. "I used to go to cellars where there were gambling games going on, with very rough people.... When I lost everything—which was quite often, since I'm so impatient ... I always thought, 'Hooray, I can go back to work.' Sometimes you lost and lost and were about to go, and then you won again, so you went on to lose some more. I was often six, seven, eight hours in these basements—and that I hated. But generally I lost and would get out very soon. And very occasionally when I won quickly I'd make a run for it." As he told Feaver, "The excitement is like nothing else: galloping home on the straight.... I'm stimulated by debt."

Freud gambled on roulette, as well as at the racetracks on dogs and horses. He was a regular at the illegal gambling nights Bacon held at his apartment, and also accompanied Bacon on gambling jaunts in London and in Monte Carlo, where Bacon lived for four years. He traveled with Graham Sutherland on one trip to visit Bacon there, during which Lucian "symbolically released caged birds from hotel windows all the way to the South."

Freud's gambling compulsion—like his womanizing—never really let up. In the 1960s, Freud owed the Kray twins—Reggie and Ronnie, infamous London gangsters and racketeers—half a million dollars. As Freud told Martin Gayford: "I liked Ronnie, not Reggie. I thought he was just a thug. But Ronnie said interesting things, although he was, as everybody knows, a sadistic murderer." In the 1980s, he was blacklisted at various racecourses for failing to pay a 19,000-pound debt. Nonetheless, he painted and became fast friends with one of his bookmakers, Victor Chandler. (When William Acquavella became his dealer in 1992, one of his first missions was to settle Freud's gambling debt of 2.7 million pounds.)

Like Bacon (and most gamblers), Freud always played for broke. He never "still had some money stashed away somewhere—I always went all out," he told Smee. "The idea of it being a sport seemed to me insane. The thing I liked was risking everything. Losing everything to do with money. And walking back from these gambling places — absolutely springing along! I loved the risk!"

Freud learned from Bacon to apply that sense of total risk to his work. Up until then, he had lived it, but not painted it. As he told Gayford, "Francis used to say that what he enjoyed most of all was 'an atmosphere of threat.'" He credited Bacon with helping him "feel more daring." He would never again return to his earlier, careful, inhibited style.

Bacon's spontaneity in everything he approached was a revelation for Freud. "I was impressed by his work, but his personality affected me. . . . He talked a great deal about the paint itself carrying the form, and imbuing the paint with this sort of life. He talked about packing a lot of things into one single brushstroke, which amused and excited me, and I realized it was a million miles from anything I could ever do. The idea of paint having that power was something, which made me feel I ought to get to know it in a different way that wasn't subservient. I mean I used to make it always do the same things for me: I'd felt I'd got a method which was acceptable and that I was getting approval for something that wasn't of great account," Freud told Feaver.

Freud understood the psychological roots of his need for radical change. "Although I'm not very introspective, I think that all this had an emotional basis. It was to do with questioning myself as a result of the way my life was going. I felt more discontented than daring. It wasn't that I was abandoning something dear to me, more that I wanted to develop something unknown to me . . . I didn't want my work to lean on anyone in particular. I wanted it to be true to me . . ."

When Freud spoke of the "emotional basis," he may have been speaking of his relationship with Caroline, which, after three years of hard living (and addictive gambling) in Soho, had begun to play itself out.

Nothing could have made that more clear than the final painting he did of her, *Hotel Bedroom,* done during an interlude in Paris in 1954; soon afterwards it was shown at the Venice Biennale. If the quartet he did of her was a musical movement, this could be considered the crescendo. It shows Freud, a shadowy ghost of a man, standing in a hotel window with a barren view of the building opposite, a tortured expression on his face, as he looks down on a prone figure on the bed, blankets drawn close to her chin, fingers anxiously caressing her cheek. It's Caroline Blackwood, looking almost corpse-like, although her glazed eyes are open. While this is also Caroline as a quintessential "girl in a bed," the transformation from the radiant, idealized image of the earlier painting with that title is extraordinary. Only the rumpled sheets connect the two. This portrait is pure film noir.

Anne Dunn thought that it was painted in their old room at the Hotel La Louisiane, during "the coldest winter in history. Caroline was frozen, and depressed by then. She knew her marriage was starting to get unfixed at that time." (Caroline herself said she was cold because Freud had broken the window to make room to paint.) There have been many interpretations: that Caroline had had a miscarriage, that she was drunk. The picture recalls Freud's painting of Kitty Garman, *Ill in Paris.* Whatever else it was, it represented a dramatic turning point in Freud's artistic life. "My eyes were completely going mad, sitting down and not being able to move. Small brushes, fine canvas. Sitting down used to drive me more and more agitated. I felt I wanted to free myself from this way of working. *Hotel Bedroom* is the last painting where I was sitting down; when I stood up, I never sat down again," he explained to Feaver.

As he told Gowing, "My awareness that I wanted to work in a different way was fired by a period of unhappiness that made it impossible for me any longer to paint sitting down. You know how you can't sit down when you are unhappy? I was aware that my work wasn't a vehicle for my feelings. . . . No, that is not quite right. I didn't want my work to carry feelings in an expressionist way. I had never questioned before that my way was the only way I could work. I saw there was something wrong about the distance between how I felt and the way I was working."

What he did instead revolutionized his work from that point on. Standing up to paint was the first step. A few years later, he began using hog-hair paintbrushes, instead of the fine sable-hair brushes he had used before. And he eventually began using a heavy lead paint called Kremnitz white, a pigment that he could make "work for me just as flesh does."

Although Francis Bacon and Caroline, who became quite close when she was married to Lucian, would remain lifelong friends, by the 1970s the famously close pair of figurative artists would finally fall out. Several factors would converge to end the friendship. Freud told Smee that he stopped talking to Bacon for several years after seeing how badly his friend had been brutalized by Bacon's then lover, a fighter pilot. Some time later, Freud refused to loan a painting that he had hanging in Dorset, *Two Figures* (of two males wrestling or more likely copulating, familiarly known as "The Buggers"), to the Tate for Bacon's second retrospective in 1985.

The two former friends traded insults through their mutual friend, Michael Wishart. When Bacon went to the Freud retrospective at the Hayward Gallery, in 1974, he remarked to Wishart, "Well, Lucian's extremely gifted but I've never been interested in Expressionism." He also said, "Everything Lucian does is so careful." Freud, in return, told Wishart that he wouldn't see Bacon "because his conversation is so repetitive." Bacon responded that he didn't want to see Freud because "his work is too repetitive." Bacon later said that they had been close, but "our ties became overstretched." As Freud put it to Smee, "when my work started being successful, Francis became bitter and bitchy."

Annie Freud recalls spending time with her father and Bacon at Wheeler's during the 1970s: "In a funny way, Dad and Francis used to behave like they were the Goncourt brothers, and tell fantastic scabrous, scandalous stories." She remembers one night, when

> Francis was there, and Dad was there and he was telling a story about being in Paris, when he hung out with Giacometti and Picasso and all these different people. And they were all talking about all the kinds of girls they liked. And one of them said that he didn't like girls who really really liked him, he preferred girls who didn't like him all that much because it was so difficult when somebody really liked you and he preferred girls that didn't like him very much and apparently Giacometti's younger brother Diego, said *"Moi, je prefer la chevre.* Me, I prefer the goat." And that's the sort of conversation they had. It was flashy, it was like being at the theater. It was like a kind of public verbal love-making — telling stories, and being absolutely scandalous and looking fantastic, and attracting attention and showing off. They were together a lot. Dinner after dinner after dinner after dinner.

Of their relationship, she says, "There was a deep love.... The friendship was extremely physical. I'll tell you something that Dad said about Francis that was so lovely. He said he had the most sensuous forearms. That is lover-like, isn't it?" Asked if they ever had sex, she says simply, "Why wouldn't they? It's there — to have."

According to Annie, the friendship ultimately soured because, in part, "I think that they both lived in a very, very gossipy world, and I think Dad began to be critical of Francis, and Francis of course heard, and was terribly wounded."

Still, the painted record of the strength of their relationship remains, brilliant and indisputable.

By 1954, Lucian Freud was a celebrated artist, although up until then he had had only a few shows, including two at the Lefevre gallery, in 1944 and 1946. Along with Francis Bacon and Ben Nicholson, he represented Britain at the 27th Venice Biennale. Twenty-two of his works were shown; in addition to *Hotel Bedroom,* they included *Girl with a Kitten, Interior in Paddington, Girl with a White Dog,* and *Francis Bacon.*

Freud was asked to write something on his work for *Encounter* magazine, and "Some Thoughts on Painting" appeared in their July edition. His comments speak forcefully about his aspirations. And, although he later claimed to regret his opening statement, in all likelihood it accurately reflects how he felt at the time:

> My object in painting pictures is to try and move the senses by giving an intensification of reality. Whether this can be achieved depends on how intensely the painter understands and feels for the person, or object of his choice. . . . The painter makes real to others his innermost feelings about all that he cares for. A secret becomes known to everyone who views the picture through the intensity with which it is felt. . . . The painter's obsession with his subject is all that he needs to drive him to work . . .

His description of his process of observation makes his ultimate goal — the same goal as psychoanalysis — crystal clear: the subject will "eventually reveal the all":

> Painters who use life itself as their subject-matter, working with the object in front of them, do so in order to translate life into art almost literally, as it were. The subject must be kept under closest

observation: if this is done, day and night, the subject — he, she
or it — will eventually reveal the all without which selection itself
is not possible: they will reveal it through some and every facet
of their lives or lack of life, through movements and attitudes,
through every variation one moment from another. It is this very
knowledge of life which can give art complete independence
from life, an independence that is necessary because the picture
in order to move us must never merely remind us of life, but must
acquire a life of its own, precisely in order to reflect life . . .

Certainly Caroline had revealed her unhappiness — if it needed
revealing — in *Hotel Bedroom*. In 1956, she left Lucian, fleeing
to Italy. Her reasons for leaving were manifold, but she later described one key dinner scene as her trigger for abandoning the
marriage.

As she told *Town and Country* in 1993, "I left him over something that wasn't anything, that was nothing, but also everything. I'm a good cook, and I'd spent all day shopping and then
cooking a perfect dinner, and then Lucian just pushed this per-
fectly cooked *rouget* back at me. If somebody offers you something, you should take the plate and then leave it if you wish — I
mean, Lucian would never eat when things weren't going well
with his work — but don't push it back. When he did, I went
out and booked into a hotel, any hotel, and that was it."

She elaborated: "There were other problems: Lucian liked
to gamble with a Dostoyevskian passion. He played Russian
roulette with everything; there was nothing he didn't take a
risk on, and it was too much for his partner. Even in his driv-
ing, he had to overtake every blind corner, risking head-ons.
That applied to his work as well." And, she added, almost as an
afterthought, she had been very young when she married and
wanted to be alone and to travel. As she told Michael Kimmel-

man, "Lucian and I couldn't be married, not endlessly. We were both too restless."

Lucian Freud was not used to being left; he was used to leaving. He couldn't accept that Caroline had actually abandoned him. "Lucian followed me. For the longest time I couldn't make him understand that I wasn't coming back," she said. "He got Francis to intervene and try to prevail on me to return to him. After I saw Francis, he explained to Lucian, 'Things end, and this has ended.' I love the idea of Francis in the role of marriage counselor."

There was another probable cause, conscious or not: Caroline wanted children, and would go on to have four — three girls and a boy — with other partners. She later remarked, "Freud was not the sort of man one could have children with." The reason for the divorce, filed one year later, was "mental cruelty."

In his book *Sacred Monsters,* Daniel Farson recounts a telling exchange with Caroline. "Have you ever driven with Lucian?" she asked Farson. "Yes, I was so terrified that when he stopped at a red light, for once, I threw myself out," Farson responded. "Exactly," said Caroline. "That's what being married to him was like."

As Freud later told Feaver, "In art you take a risk. It's actually a deliberate thing. You are on the diving board. And in life it's even slightly difficult to define what is a risk. Unless you are playing, like I used to, Russian roulette with motor cars. You know: dashing across the road with your eyes shut to test your luck. In working, one of the things that makes you continue and is a stimulant is the difficulty surely?"

But in life, that difficulty eventually takes a toll.

7

Carnal Knowledge

B Y ALL ACCOUNTS, Freud was devastated when Caroline left him. Indeed, some of those closest to him feared he might commit suicide. Charles Lumley, a friend who also worked as the artist's longtime assistant, once recalled, "We were worried he might top himself. . . . I was asked to look after him by his friends. I remember Bacon being terrified that Lu might go on the balcony and throw himself off. Lu was in a really bad way." When Freud refused to return to the house on Dean Street where he and Caroline had lived, Lumley had to rescue some of the paintings.

After his second marriage ended, Lucian never married again. He spent the period after Caroline's departure "getting up to things to do with girls, chasing around a lot and dancing and nightclubbing and parties, and dice games and Soho," he told Feaver. And of course, a lot of gambling.

Freud's gambling at the time caused a final rift with his brother Clement, with whom he had never been close. Apart from their childhood sibling rivalry, the two had had an early, bitter falling out when, racing each other through a park, Lucian prevented Clement from winning by shouting "Stop thief!" causing passersby to intervene. Although he hadn't seen his brother in years, that didn't stop Lucian from seeking a loan for his gambling debts in 1955. When Lucian went to Clement's private club to ask for the money, "Clement refused to lend, so that was it," Charles Lumley recalled.

Although eventually Clement became famous as a broadcaster, writer, and member of Parliament, Freud never spoke to him again, nor did he attend his funeral when he died in 2009. He even said he turned down a knighthood because Clement had received one. "My younger brother has one of those. That's all that needs to be said of the matter." (As Freud later told an interviewer, "My younger brother Clement has become a very public figure. He's a household word in London . . . he lectures, he writes, he's a TV personality, he makes dog food commercials. . . . I can't really tolerate him.")

Freud's transition to a more "daring" painterly style would take place gradually over the next several years. In 1956, he stopped using fine sable brushes and began using a hog-hair brush, which enabled him to apply paint with far more flexibility and force.

Eventually, he began to introduce his trademark pile of painter's rags into his compositions, as well as his studio's floorboards. In effect, he was doing something almost counter-intuitive to his obsessive personality: he was experimenting. "You long to do something that doesn't look like your own work — something that frees you from your own nature," he said later.

Most critics identify Freud's 1958–59 painting, *Woman Smiling,* as his leap into a new creative realm. He himself told Gowing that he considered this portrait a major turning point. As Gowing puts it, "It was in the portrait of a woman, where most things happen in Freud's work, that the breakthrough came. With *Woman Smiling,* the constructive energy was liberated." As John Russell observed: "The looser, more fatty to-and-fro of the brush marked a complete break with the perfected enamel of a year or two before."

The mottling that had already been introduced in his portraits of Caroline, *Girl Reading* and *Girl in Bed,* was taken to a
whole new level in this portrait of his current model and lover,
Suzy Boyt. For the first time, the paint on Freud's canvases had
heft, both literal and figurative. A sculptural, rather than illustrative approach, forcibly emerged. This new direction had already been suggested in several works from the previous year or
so, *Woman in a White Shirt* (1956–57) and even more visibly in
A Young Painter (1957–58), but it came to fruition in *Woman
Smiling.* Freud had begun to explore the pure power of paint as
a medium, rather than painting as if he were drawing.

The difference was palpable. "These wedges of color were
expressions of purpose in the paint and in the flesh, the paint
that was driven across the surface with the springy bristles of
the hog-hair brush quite unlike the brushes of the pliant sable,
which had followed the form with obedient literalness," wrote
Gowing. "Freud's work has been concerned with this kind of
impulse ever since, with the fullness of form and the bodily life
shining through it. . . . The sensuousness and the material rich-
ness, which Freud had set his face against as a youth, were suddenly at his disposal in altogether new forms, quite energetic."

As for the handling of the paint itself, "The brush comes
sweeping down, zigzagging cross the canvas. . . . It describes great
churning curves which make the form, recreate the pose and
impulsively enact, as it seems, the expression." Freud was learning that to imbue art with a sense of life, exaggeration is often a
more powerful tool than exactitude.

Not surprisingly, when Freud deliberately veered away from
his meticulous drawing style, everything in his art became larger
and looser. "I had stopped drawing and worked with bigger
brushes," Freud himself explained. The "bigger" also applied
to scale; most of Freud's works in the 1960s were literally larger
than life. The artist had entered a dynamic new phase of his ca-

reer, one that he would vigorously pursue until the end of his life.

Freud's personal life was also changing: he had entered into several new overlapping romantic relationships. He had begun teaching part time at the Slade School of Fine Art in 1949; for years after that he was a visiting tutor. Arguably, Freud got much more from the school than he gave: Suzy Boyt was one of several art students he would meet at Slade who would bear him children. (Another facet of his risk taking was his never using protection or birth control with his lovers.)

Suzy gave birth to Alexander Boyt, known as Ali, in 1957, the same year that the divorce with Caroline was finalized, making it likely that Lucian was involved with Suzy while still married to Blackwood. Their twelve-year liaison would produce three more children: Rose and Susie, born in 1958 and 1969, respectively, both of whom became novelists, and Isobel, born in 1961, now a teacher. Boyt also had a son, Kai, by an earlier marriage, whom Freud treated as a stepson.

Freud was not much more than an occasional presence during most of the childhoods of his offspring. As he himself put it, "I like them when I can talk to them and take them out. I never thought, 'Ooh, what a lovely baby.'" Nonetheless, he did portraits of several of his children as infants, starting with the drawing of Kitty cradling his first child, Annie (*Mother and Baby,* 1949).

"He was painting most of the time, obviously, but he used to come around to see us as a family and take us out to supper," Rose Boyt has said. When she was fifteen and left home, he used to stop by her flat, "and we used to just talk. I suppose that's when I started to know him more as an adult." Rose also recalls learning about poetry from Lucian. "I went from seeing him a handful of times a year to three or four times a week. We talked all the time, we got to know each other, discovered we had a lot in common, liked a lot of the same things. He used to make really delicious things to eat."

Still, in her novel, *Rose,* published in 1992, one gets a sense of the distance she may have felt as a child. "My father's car was as long as a hearse. It used to make me sick riding in the back of it. I would watch my color changing out of the corner of my eye in the small slanted mirrors that lured me, as they gleamed in their padded alcoves beside the back windows, with the splendor of their very existence. . . . I saw myself fading and knew, by the time I was taking my seat opposite my father at the table of the restaurant, that my face was green . . ."

The feeling of loss is also evoked in the next passage: "He held me in his arms at a tall window that overlooked a square and trees. He was singing to me. You great big beautiful doll. Let me put my arms around you, I'm so glad I found you. My mother was washing a lettuce under a running tap. My brother and sister were sitting at the table, my sister in a high chair, waiting for lunch. You great big beautiful doll. That was me. My father was holding me in his arms. I was sitting on his forearm, my legs dangling, looking out the window. Then he put me down and slipped away."

Suzy, who had given up painting, sold vintage clothes at her own shop and later at an antiques market. Clearly something of an adventurer, she at one point bought a ship and took her four children out of school to sail around the world, dropping anchor in Trinidad, where they settled for a while. (Rose also writes about that experience, and of her mother's affair with the captain, in her novel.) Lucian was entirely absent during these escapades.

Susie, the youngest Boyt child, was named after her mother at Lucian's suggestion. "I realized from an early age what he was about," Susie has said of her father. "That he drank, slept and breathed paint. When you're extremely good at something — as he was — every day becomes a bit of a crisis. And much of his existence was about trying to work that out. He was the only father I had so I got in with it and tried to enjoy it. . . . He had an amazing capacity to inspire love in those who knew him. It was something so marked you couldn't ignore it."

Unbekownst to Suzy Boyt, more or less at the same time Freud was very seriously involved with Katherine McAdam, whom he had first met when she was nineteen, in about 1952, before his marriage to Caroline Blackwood. After he and Caroline divorced, the relationship resumed, and then continued for about fifteen years. Their first child, a daughter, Jane, was born in 1958. Three more children would follow in fairly short order: Paul, born in 1959, Lucy, in 1961, and David in 1964.

According to Jane, who gives a candid account of Freud as a father in those early years, he met her mother when he attended a dance at St. Martin's art school, where Katherine, who was studying fashion, was formally announced as the belle of the ball. They quickly became involved. Katherine had no idea that Freud was also seeing Caroline Blackwood, and, Jane recalls, "was just devastated" when she read in the paper that Freud had gotten married. (For a time, Katherine had worked as a baby sitter for Freud's first wife, Kitty Garman, tending to Annie and Annabel.)

After Freud's divorce in 1957, "He came back to her absolutely devastated and she had to take care of him," Jane says. "He came to my mom to find a nurturer, so she took him back. He was very needy." When Jane was born, "he found us a place in Paddington, close to his studio, and he was living with us on and off, because he was painting at night." Jane, herself a serious artist, recalls, "I remember that's when he gave me the most attention, when I was drawing."

But as Jane got older, things began to disintegrate. "They must have argued toward the end, because my most vivid memories are him saying, 'Jane, get your Mom, she won't let me in,' so he had to go back to his studio. 'Tell her I'm here,' he would say, 'please try to persuade her,' and I couldn't. I remember him camping outside on the doorstep and seeing him there when I went to school in the morning, and it just felt terrible because he would stay there all night, and she wouldn't let him in."

When Jane was eight, Katherine reached the end of her tolerance for Freud's extreme philandering. By then she had realized that his nights away were not only spent "painting." Without a word to Lucian, she simply packed the children up and moved them out to council housing in southwest London, leaving no forwarding address. "We weren't able to say goodbye. I felt so bad because I thought he would think I had left him. I was just gutted in the removal van that he wouldn't be able to find us," Jane says of this traumatic experience.

The four children were not only wrenched away from their familiar surroundings, they were also wrenched away from their grandparents, Ernst and Lucie, who lived nearby, and whom Jane saw on a daily basis: they picked her up from the school bus every day and took her home for tea. "They were just so kind to me," she recalls. "Lucie would ask me about school and serve these little cups of tea with bone china saucers, and Danish pastries. Ernst was this amazing presence, always with her in the room."

Jane and her siblings would not see their father again until they were adults. Like the various other Freud children, Jane had no way to reach him, since he didn't give his phone number or address even (or especially) to his own parents. Lucian apparently made no effort to communicate with them. Katherine never saw him again.

Jane reunited with her father when she was thirty-one, but her other three siblings didn't really communicate with him again until years later, when he was on his deathbed. As Lucy recalled, "Mum never talked about him ever. Over the years we seemed to lose our heritage and I was known by Mum's surname, McAdam. . . . I always knew that my dad was a famous artist. I grew to accept that we didn't see him, it was just the way it was." She had seen him once in her twenties, as did the other McAdams' (who had been dubbed by the media "the forgotten Freuds") over lunches facilitated by Esther, her half-sister, whom she had finally met after her brother David had serendipitously encountered their cousin Emma, Clement's daughter. But he didn't respond when Lucy invited him to her wedding, or when she sent him a pamphlet with a portrait she had done of him.

Meanwhile, in about 1959, Freud had also started a relationship with another young woman, only eighteen at the time, Bernadine Coverley, who would bear him two daughters, Bella and Esther. Since the tender, lovely portrait of her, *Pregnant Girl,* was done in 1960–61, one assumes he probably met her in about 1959. But even with her face averted from the artist, her resemblance to her older daughter, Bella, born in 1961, is notable. Freud soon painted a picture of the baby, *Bella on a Green Sofa* (1961), the inevitable sequel to *Pregnant Girl.*

As Esther, born two years later, in 1963, wrote in her mother's obituary (shockingly, since she was a full twenty years younger, her death occurred just four days after Lucian's, in July, 2011): "By the late 1950's she had already discovered Soho and the night clubs of Notting Hill, and caught a glimpse of Lucian Freud." Remarkably, although Freud would become most famous for his explicit nudes, his portrait of her was one of the first nudes he painted, if only from the breasts up. It would be five more years, when the artist was in his mid-forties, before he would attempt his first full-scale nude.

Like Suzy, Bernadine, described as "a writer, gardener and free spirit," took her children on an exotic adventure: Esther's first novel, *Hideous Kinky,* which later became a movie starring Kate Winslet and Harvey Keitel, tells the tale of their trip to

Morocco. There are glancing mentions of an absent father in London, who rarely sends money, and never on time. ("I absolutely don't have a penny. What with your father and the Moroccan postal service, it's a wonder anything ever gets through at all," her fictional mother sobs.) Esther later recalled a rare visit when she was seven, and the "vivid" impression Lucian made in his ritzy car, probably his beloved Bentley. "He had not been with my mother since I was born. . . . He was glamorous, elegant and from a different world. He told me recently he wasn't very interested in babies or children."

It wasn't until she moved to London when she was sixteen and began to model for him that she had something of a regular relationship with her father. As she said in a documentary made by Jake Auerbach (Frank's son) in 2004, "You have a choice, and not all of his children have made it, from very young, that you can get the good bit if you want to accept what he's like. Or you cannot get it by being angry for him not being like someone else's father. . . . When I was sixteen, I moved to London, and almost immediately I started to sit for him. And it was a really lovely way of getting to know him because until then I hadn't ever lived in the same city as him." Indeed, for Freud's children, posing for him was their only real opportunity for closeness.

At the same time, hovering in the background of all these other relationships was his long-term affair with Belinda Lambton ("Bindy"), whom he first painted in 1960. According to her daughter, Lucinda, Bindy was Freud's mistress for "many, many, many, many years." (Indeed, it was Freud's relationship with Bindy and her husband, Tony Lambton, that caused Kitty and her second husband, Wynne Godley, to take Freud to court when Annie was an adolescent. "It was very damaging," Annie recalls.)

Lady Jane Willoughby was another serious long-term lover. (She is depicted in *Head* [1962]; *Woman in a Fur Coat,* a

thoughtful portrait of her clad in leopard, was painted in 1967.)
And Freud would have two more relationships that produced
known children, one with Lady Jacquetta Eliot, Countess of
St. Germans, who had a son, Freddy, in 1971, and one with the
painter Celia Paul, whose son, Frank, was born in 1985, and who
was the painter's muse for several years in the 1980s, and the
subject of some of his most memorably touching nudes.

"I have several children strewn about. But I only get the
pleasure out of them. I take them out or go to see them. Basi-
cally I'm a loner. I do as I please," Freud told the writer John
Gruen in 1977. At last count, Freud had fourteen acknowledged
children. He jokingly called himself "one of the great absentee
fathers of the age."

Carola Zentner recalled her mother going to a private view
of one of Lucian's shows in about 1970, and Lucian's mother,
Lucie, nudging her and saying, "'You see that young man over
there? I think that's one of Lucian's children.' My mother said,
'how do you know'?' And Lucie said, 'Well, he just turned to
Lucian and said 'Dad.'"

Annie, his first daughter by Kitty, and the oldest of Freud's
children, has strong, fond memories of her father from when
she was a toddler right up through her early teens. "I did have a
proper childhood, not quite, not a live-in dad, but the next-best
thing," she says. Indeed, when she and her sister Annabel were
very young, they spent time not just with their father, but with
Lucian and Caroline.

"When I was about three and a half, I remember very well
the smell of my father. He smelled of paint and turpentine," she
says. "I remember the house we lived in in Maida Vale, near St.
John's Wood, near his parents' house. I remember him grabbing
my hand when we used to run across the road, pulling me so I
would run, not endangering life and limb, but communicating
to me a sort of enjoyment of risk that continued always through

my childhood. He drew me within a few weeks of my being born. And I remember him painting me — he painted me all the way through my childhood. He was a very big part of my life." Annie, a respected poet, shared a deep love of poetry with her father, who constantly quoted from memory T. S. Eliot, William Butler Yeats, John Berryman, and A. E. Housman.

Annie has astute observations regarding Freud's public persona, from his apparent levity about gambling to his attitude towards parenting: "There weren't many like him, somebody of that magnitude of genius if you like. There's something that people don't factor in . . . which is the notion of a person's mythology about themselves. It's terribly important and it's how they keep anxiety at bay in order to be able to dedicate themselves so dangerously to their art. . . . My dad used to talk to me very, very light-heartedly about gambling, and indeed he did with I think everybody that he was intimately close to. But I could see, because I went through it as a child, the agony of the stress that he put himself under. He talked about gambling and losing absolutely everything, and I mean absolutely everything. I mean money that was not just his own, but that belonged to other people, He used to call it 'cleaning himself out' as if it was something kind of salutary. But I could see that it was agony and terrifying."

On the other hand, she continues, "Dad had this way of intensifying all the things that he was obsessive about." It was, she says:

> an aspect of behavior that might be terribly weird and freaky to the person trying to make sense of him, but would just kind of be ordinary for him. And it's important to try and make distinctions between the created self and the unchosen self. For example, he said to me sometimes, "You know I'm just a painting machine." But he did learn how to do that. He taught himself not to need sleep.

If he had a condition, it was the kind of condition that very, very amazing philosophers might have, where they construct the world so that they just don't see that it's simply dreadful to love somebody and then to love many other people and many other people and many other people. Because it is dreadful. . . . I know that he was phobic about other people's passions. Particularly if they were expressed in a way that placed pressure and demands on him.

When I was younger, I was in a great deal of suffering about him. But I don't feel that anymore, for many, many reasons, reasons to do with him, to do with me, my development, my success as a writer. But I remember when I was in my say late twenties, early thirties . . . and had given birth to my daughter here, and met brother and sister after brother and sister, there were several occasions when there was discussion about the upbringing of children, and he would quite often talk about this matter. And I remember experiencing tremendous rage that he seemed to have the most extraordinary level of perceptiveness and interest and subtleness of inquiry, if you like, when he had been so absolutely remiss himself. . . . I found it quite awful. Because it felt like the absolute last laugh. He could feel it emotionally, but he wouldn't carry it out, except when he chose to. That's what I am trying to say . . . about a moral system that is constructed so that he can live his life.

In a 2006 interview with Freud, Sebastian Smee asked him if he had fallen in love many times. "No!" Freud replied, going on to explain that, contrary to outward appearances, "I don't think so. I think about two or three times. Which is about as much as is possible, I think. People go on and talk about it every day, but I think it's comparatively rare. I'm not talking about habits, nor am I talking about hysterics. I'm talking about actual, completely absolute concern, where everything about the other person interests, worries or pleases you."

Freud's canvas came between him and true intimacy with

any of this extraordinary circle of lovers and children. Painting always indisputably came first. Towards the end of his life, Freud was asked, "What makes you paint?" The artist responded succinctly: "It is what I like doing best and I am completely selfish."

8

Channeling Courbet

IN 1960 AND 1961, Freud traveled briefly to Holland and France; Bindy Lambton accompanied him on some of these trips, and modeled for him in 1960, when he painted *Head on a Green Sofa,* and in 1961, *Figure with Bare Arms* (1961–62). "A spectacular shape and famous for it. She had this amazing discipline over her hips," Freud observed, although the latter portrait emphasizes her bust, in a close-fitting white shirt.

Freud went abroad to see several art works and exhibits: specifically Hals, Ingres, Goya, and Courbet. (Courbet's *L'Origine du Monde,* a lush female nude shown from one partially exposed breast down, her luxuriant pubic hair and labia fully exposed, is still the art world's ne plus ultra for sexual shock value; painted in 1866, it could not even be publicly shown until 1988.) He spent two days at Montpellier: "I looked at the Courbets and (those Géricault limbs) a lot ... I like Courbet. His shamelessness." "Shamelessness" was also a quality Freud had admired in Bacon and for which he would become notorious in his own work.

When Delamere Terrace was torn down in 1962, Freud moved to Clarendon Crescent. "At Clarendon I was painting 4 a.m. to lunch, then off gambling. Lot of playing, day and night, horses and dogs, I was completely broke," he later said. The new studio, like the old one, was a condemned terrace along the canal. "It was known as Bug Alley: had to be debugged before I moved in," Freud recalled to Feaver. For Freud, it was also reminiscent of "Doré's London." Long and narrow, the upper floor space (with a lavatory on the balcony) imposed its own restrictions, and Freud knocked down a wall to open it up.

The portraits he painted there reflect his new approach; *Red-Haired Man on a Chair* (1962–63), a painting of his friend and Slade student Tim Behrens, looks almost Baconesque in its torqued perspective. Behind him, mid-canvas, runs a rough dirty white river — Freud's painting rags, plastered up against the wall. They intersect with the post, creating a strange cruciform, perhaps another nod to Bacon. This is one of the first times Freud used rags as a compositional element in a painting; they would become a well-known motif.

Freud's *Sleeping Head* (1962), chin leaning on shoulder, face averted from the viewer so it is almost featureless, was also something of a watershed for the painter. The extreme, unfocussed close-up of a woman's broadly painted head, both in its scale and ductility, served as a model for Freud's future endeavors. "I was going to do a nude," Freud explained to Gowing: "Then I realized I could do it from the head." It was a form of synecdoche on canvas, later to be fully realized in Freud's famously expansive nudes.

The loosely painted head of John Deakin (1963–64), the photographer and Colony Room regular, is miles away in technique from the tautly rendered head Freud had done of John Minton, another Colony Room member, a decade earlier. *Man's Head Self-Portrait* (1963), painted in long, loose strokes, in a foreshortened perspective perhaps caused either by the tight quarters Freud was working in, or the fact that he is looking down into a mirror, seems like a study for his later self-portrait, *Reflection with Two Children, Self-Portrait* (1965), painted in an unusual grey palette, which also evokes Bacon. In it, Freud towers above two tiny children almost lost in the lower left-hand corner, Ali and Rose Boyt. The brutally raw *Man and His*

Daughter (1963–64) of a badly scarred neighbor, Ted, "a very clever bank robber," and his daughter Sharon, is another arresting work to emerge from this time.

In October, 1963, Freud had his second show at Marlborough Galleries; his first had been in the spring of 1958. Twenty-four works were exhibited, including *Woman Smiling, Sleeping Head,* the portrait of Bernadine, called *Nude with Dark Hair* (it was later changed to *Pregnant Girl*), *Baby on a Green Sofa, Naked Child Laughing,* and *Red-Haired Man — Interior* (later changed to *Red-Haired Man on a Chair*).

Freud's new work was not instantly admired; both shows turned out to be a very hard sell. "Shown a year or two later, the new pictures were greeted with something like consternation," Gowing wrote, in what was probably an understatement. "The pictures that Freud began when he was thirty were a drastic reversal of what was expected of him."

Kenneth Clark, for one, former director of the National Gallery and a strong early supporter, personally expressed his disgust with the new work to Freud. "After the exhibition opened he wrote a card saying that I had deliberately suppressed everything that made my work remarkable, or something like that, and ended, 'I admire your courage.' I never saw him again," Freud later recalled.

Until now, Freud had focused on clothed models ("I am inclined to think of them [humans] . . . if they are dressed as animals dressed up," he once said) and heads (often in close-up). Although in 1950 he did a portrait called *Sleeping Nude* in the same style as his Kitty portraits (and in fact this probably is Kitty), her body is covered from the hips down; and her cold, pure, marble-tinted torso and head have a whiff as much of death as sleep. In 1963 Freud did a painting of his eldest daughter, fifteen-year-old Annie, *Naked Child Laughing,* but, because she is cold, embarrassed, or both, she is hugging herself, essentially covering her nudity. It barely hints at what was to come.

Appointed a visiting tutor at Norwich art school in 1964, Freud instructed his students to paint naked self-portraits (provoking protests from some parents). "I want you to try to make the most revealing, telling and believable object," he ordered them. "Something really shameless, you know." The artist also clearly aimed the assignment at himself.

In 1965, when the Clarendon space was demolished, Freud moved studios again, this time to 227 Gloucester Terrace, also in Paddington, where he would remain until 1972. And it was there, in 1966, that he did his first full-fledged nude, *Naked Girl,* embarking on the decades-long series of radical female nudes that would seal Freud's reputation as "the greatest living realist painter."

Seen from the new foreshortened downward angle, the slender blonde model — who also appears in *Naked Girl Asleep* (1967 and 1968) — is lying on a richly rumpled white sheet, her not particularly erotic genitalia anchoring the center of the composition, although her legs are tightly closed. Her arms are flung upwards, and her face is tilted back, half-asleep.

For the first time, Freud did not focus on the sitter's head; he specifically chose to consider the head "as a limb." "I wanted very deliberately the figure not to be strengthened by the head," he told Feaver. This strategy would prove to be a key element in the power of Freud's many subsequent nudes; his portraits were to be of the entire body, with no more painterly attention given to the head than to an arm. In fact, Freud preferred the term "naked portraits" to nudes. And naked they were.

"I'm really interested in them as animals," Freud would later say. "Part of liking to work from them naked is for that reason. Because I can see more: see the forms repeating right through the body and often in the head as well. One of the most exciting things is seeing through the skin, to the blood and veins and markings."

Freud painted the model (Penelope Cuthbertson, according to *Vanity Fair*, which referred to her as "one of the most lusted-after birds of swinging London and now married to the Honorable Desmond Guinness") again in 1967 and then in 1968: both paintings (one is in close-up) called *Naked Girl Asleep*, this time in a more athletic pose, her arms and legs akimbo, yet still somehow not sexually suggestive. "That whole series was known as 'Penny's Parts,'" a female friend of Freud's once commented. "Because there are so many parts, aren't there?" But that snippy observation totally misses the point. There is nothing prurient about Freud's intense examination of his nude model in these pivotal paintings; it is, however, clinically thorough, in the way a doctor's or veterinarian's might be.

"My grandfather was adamant that to be an analyst you had to be a fully qualified medical doctor, and whenever he examined any of his patients whatever desperate state they were in he gave them a complete and thorough physical examination. That seems to me right and proper," Freud has said. Indeed, to a certain extent, Freud considered himself "a biologist," and John Richardson has remarked that it was his grandfather's early interest in *biology*, not psychology, that was most influential in Freud's work.

As the art historian Sir John Rothenstein remarked, "The art of Lucian Freud is the product of a long unblinking stare — a stare without warmth, without illusions, a stare above all of sheer fascination." A fascination without boundaries.

In the coming years Freud would paint a masterly and minutely attentive series of his depressed and ailing mother. He would also paint explicit nudes of most of his daughters and one son, nude portraits of his aging self, nudes of several enormous models that focus on their fleshy amplitude, and nude portraits of his studio assistant, David Dawson. (In fact, his very last painting is of Dawson, nude, with his whippet, Eli.)

"I'm very conscious of whether I've got a naked man or na-ked woman in front of me. Sometimes I can't stop. Like those cars that get so hot that when you turn the engine off it goes on banging away," he said. Taking a cue from Courbet, Freud cre-ated work that was uniquely his own.

9

Intimations of Mortality

FROM MIDCAREER ONWARD, both nudity and mortality became salient features of Freud's work. While his paintings have always exuded a certain amount of decadence, in both senses of the word, during the second half of his life, Freud poignantly documented his own aging process — and that of his mother, creating some of his most powerful paintings.

Although over the years Freud had done many self-portraits, both drawings and paintings, those he did from his forties on took on a new meaning as the passage of time became more evident. Mirrors obviously played a role in their creation — one mirror in particular, a five-foot Georgian looking-glass he hauled from 20 Delamere Terrace to every subsequent studio for the next few decades, although he also used a hand mirror.

Freud approached his portraits of himself with the same lack of sentimentality with which he approached those of his other models. "You've got to try to paint yourself as another person," Freud explained to Feaver. Still, he acknowledged, "Looking in the mirror is a strain that looking at other people isn't at all."

Using a mirror, Freud did three very similar self-portraits in 1963, two with his cheek leaning on his hand, including *Man's Head Self-Portrait*, and one that resembles a more formal sculptural bust. These led up to his strongest self-portrait to date, the remarkable *Reflection with Two Children* (1965), mentioned earlier, with its Baconesque perspective.

Three Studies for a Portrait of Lucian Freud (1964), painted by Bacon the previous year, offers a clear comparison between the two still-close painters' styles; in it Freud's red-hued face is whisked into three twisted incarnations. No matter how "daring" he became, and how many taboos he ultimately broke, Freud remained an avid realist.

The artist constantly experimented with placing both mirrors in various parts of the studio, with interesting results. *Interior with Hand Mirror* (1967) captures a miniature head of Freud in an oval mirror seemingly balanced on a window sill, a quirky composition in terms of visual planes — mirror versus window. And then there is the strikingly mysterious *Interior with Plant, Reflection, Listening* (1967–68), in which a diminutive, sharp-featured Freud peers out from behind a flourishing spiky palm tree familiar from past paintings, an illustration to an unspoken narrative.

"There have been occasional signs of proneness to a self-image of defiant isolation, bony, even dwarfish in the raking light," wrote Gowing of Freud's self-portraits. "It is the only part of his work in which his enormous mastery seems as if manipulated to fortify a posture that is defensive, with latent tones of hostility and sorrow." In *Small Interior* (self-portrait, 1968,) a rather antic, full-body Freud flourishes his brush; reflected in the Georgian mirror is his easel, with the start of a painting of his daughter Isobel, known as Ib.

Freud portrays himself as surprisingly vulnerable in some self-portraits; much less so in others, particularly those in which his children figure. His menacing absent presence in the startling portrait of seven-year-old Ib, naked from the waist down, asleep beneath an indoor tree, informs *Large Interior, Paddington* (1968); only the artist's coat, hanging in a corner, implies his masculine proximity.

Freud's father died in 1970. The artist made a rare, stern-looking pencil drawing of him several months before his death. Although Freud had never been very close to his father, he stashed a portfolio of Ernst's early watercolors, carefully preserved by his mother, in one of his studio drawers.

Around this time, Freud began a detailed but desolate painting, *Wasteground with Houses,* of buildings and abandoned rubbish seen from his studio window. He was well aware of the way, after his father's death, the piece took on much more pointed references to decay. "I felt the rubbish must be more exact; I felt somehow the rubbish was the life of the painting . . . I am fascinated with the haphazard way it has come about, with the poignancy of the impermanency of it," he told Feaver. (He also noticed that during periods of strain and upset, he tended to prefer painting "the view out the window" rather than "staring at people or bodies all day.")

In 1972, Freud moved again, this time to 19 Thorngate Road in Maida Vale. There Freud embarked on something singularly Freudian, in the most purely psychoanalytic meaning of the term; he began an intimate series of portraits of his mother, who after his father's death tried to kill herself by overdosing on pills, but was saved at the last minute by her sister, Gerda. "She didn't want to live without my father. It was absolutely clear . . . she left a note saying, 'I've gone to join him,'" Freud told Smee.

Foiled in her determined effort, Lucie never really recovered her will to live. Thus incapacitated, "a shadow of her former self," as Carola Zentner put it, she became a desirable model for Freud. For the first time, her insistent mothering no longer threatened him. And finally, he could act like an attentive son. Freud did this the only way he knew how: by painting her.

"I had a good model. But then also, I did it to cheer her up, to give her something to do," he said. Beginning in 1972, and continuing regularly for eight or nine years, he would fetch his mother in the morning, have breakfast with her at a café, and bring her to his studio to paint her; the first paintings were two close-ups of her head.

From the time he was a small boy, Freud had felt his mother to be an unbearably intrusive presence. "If my father hadn't died I'd never have painted her. I started working from her because she lost interest in me; I couldn't have if she had been interested.... She barely noticed, but I had to overcome a lifetime of avoiding her.... She was so affectionately, insistently maternal. And she preferred me.... From very early on she treated me in, in a way, as an only child. I resented her interest; I felt it was threatening. She was so intuitive. And she liked forgiving me; she forgave me for things I never even did," he told Feaver.

To a great extent Lucie adhered to the stereotype of an overbearing (Jewish) mother. "My mother was so keen on my becoming an artist, it made me feel sick," Lucian once said. According to a 2012 documentary on Freud, *Lucian Freud: Painted Life,* directed by Randall Wright, Lucie used to hoard her son's love-letters — much as she had hoarded all his early doodles and drawings. (She even wrote to his girlfriends asking for his letters.) Freud also confessed to Gowing that when he was very young, his mother used to make him give her drawing lessons, perhaps in an effort to encourage his artistic talent. As he later told Smee, "Of course, when I thought about it afterwards I blushed. Naturally at that time I didn't realize she was just trying to make more and more of a connection with me."

Caroline Blackwood claimed that when Freud was in his teens, his mother had actually bought out a small show Freud had been given. "It traumatized him — that his mother had bought everything. She didn't give anyone any time to buy them, she just zoomed in. It's an aggression really, isn't it? They had a terrific rift over that. Only late in her life did he start painting her — after she became very ill." (According to Freud she was actually in quite good health, but feigned illness.)

Freud told Gayford that Lucie would leave parcels of food for him during his days in Paddington, a habit he abhorred. As he recalled to Gruen, "She used to be a very aggressive woman. She was like that all her life, and I saw very little of her, I didn't want to see her, didn't like being with her."

Perhaps never has a fraught mother-son relationship been so obsessively — and sometimes strangely objectively — recorded. While some critics have seen Freud's portraits of his mother as tender, Blackwood and Gruen characterized them as "terrifying." Actually, they are both. "When I was painting a picture of my mother years ago, I was feeling sadder than I ever have before or since," Freud later told Gayford. "I was painting the paisley patterns on her dress and I remember worrying that my sadness would get into the paisley shapes and I suppose perhaps it did."

That did not prevent him from later merging his mother with a portrait of one of his lovers, Jacquetta Eliot (who, unbeknownst to Lucie, had borne her a grandson, Freddy, two years earlier) in the painting *Large Interior, W9* (1973). (The two did not sit together; Jacquetta was added later.) Oedipal barely begins to describe this disturbing work, one of the earliest in Freud's series of mother portraits.

In it, Lucie, dressed in drab, dark clothes, sits in a leather chair, eyes cast down. A mortar and pestle, full of dark pigment, sits on the expanse of floorboards, its rim partly beneath the chair. Behind Lucie a prone nude is stretched out in an almost odalisque pose (or the closest Freud came to it), her naked body exposed from the waist up, her arms folded behind her head, her eyes staring up at the ceiling.

There is no attempt to excise the stark sexuality of the image; one wonders what Lucie must have made of it. Although Freud never relied on symbols, preferring to paint "what was directly in front" of him, the mortar and pestle evoke a sense of creativity — artistic creativity, in that the mortar holds the pigment for the painting, but also the creativity of the phallic pestle penetrating the circular vessel's dark ooze.

Tame by comparison, the other portraits in the series remain haunting. *The Painter's Mother Reading* (1975), is a bust of Lucie, again clad in dark clothes, her downcast face sagging with age, as she peruses Freud's favorite reference book, *Geschicte Aegyptians.* It is noteworthy that although Lucie probably didn't recognize its relevance, Freud had handed her his Rosetta stone, the only book he portrayed in paint. "I made her look at the Egyptian book, but she's not registering," he told Feaver.

Between 1976 and 1977, Freud did several rather delicate, if intense, portraits of his mother in bed, wearing a paisley-printed housecoat; in *The Painter's Mother Resting I* and *II,* her hands are up by the pillow, her posture passive and helpless. In *The Painter's Mother Resting III,* one hand rests beneath her breast; her expression is beyond resignation. Frank observations of the frailness of human flesh, these portraits are as much about Freud's own mortality as his mother's.

The series reaches its culmination in *The Painter's Mother* (1982–84). Using a minimalist palette, Freud depicts his white-haired mother as a very old woman-in-white, set against an austere brown and beige background. It looks almost penitential (although whose penance isn't clear). His last portrait of his mother is a simple charcoal drawing of her done the day after she died, *The Painter's Mother Dead* (1989).

"I always wanted to be an orphan and to be completely parentless," Freud said just a few years later, adding, "And the extraordinary thing is I had a happy upbringing." Yet, as he later declared, "My mother said that my first word was *alleine,* which means 'alone.' Leave me alone."

10

Bypassing Decorum

THROUGHOUT MOST OF the fifties, sixties, and seventies, Freud operated more or less under the art world's radar. Pop art, Op art, even abstract expressionism came and went, and Freud obsessively pursued his radical version of realism, moving at his own pace from linear to dimensional, from small to large, from an inhibited tautness to a confident looseness. "I found something almost exhilarating in being forgotten, working underground," he claimed.

In 1974, Freud had his first retrospective, at the Hayward Gallery, from January 3 through March 3, accompanied by a comprehensive catalogue essay by John Russell. The show had been instigated, in part, by the eminent critic David Sylvester. As the catalogue's preface notes, although Freud had already established quite a reputation in his teens, this was actually his formal introduction to the British art-going public. Organized by the Arts Council of Great Britain, the show traveled to three other British cities: Bristol, Birmingham, and Leeds.

"Lucian was seen as Francis Bacon's sort of pet when he was at the Marlborough Gallery, under the wing of Bacon, and his work was sold to a particular group of people," notes Anthony d'Offay, who represented Freud from the 1970s through the '80s. "And then with the show at the Hayward, it really opened up, and he was seen for the first time as a painter in his own right."

Several reviews compared his oeuvre favorably to that of Edvard Munch, whose show occupied the lower floor of the gallery. Writing in the London *Times,* Paul Overy declared: "Few living artists could hold their own with the Edvard Munch exhibition downstairs. Freud does." Overy lauded the painting *Large Interior, W9* (of Freud's mother and Jacquetta) as "a remarkable achievement ... I doubt whether there is any other artist working in Britain today who could equal it."

All the reviews referred to a certain darkness in Freud's work. "Freud has penetrating insight into unhappy people," wrote Peter Stone in the *Jewish Chronicle.* "Suppressed suffering and the disquiet of the age are here in these purely autobiographical works..."

In *Connoisseur* magazine, Peter Fuller put it in more psychoanalytical terms. "Things as he sees them are always fringed with menace, with a claustrophobic dream-like angst," Fuller wrote, focusing on a key facet of Freud's work: the level of transference that occurred during the painting process, which Freud himself called a "transaction." "We come to conclude that the anxiety which he sees in so much around him — which characterises all his pictures of people — derives not so much from that which he has seen as from that which he has projected on what he has seen — the pain within himself that he will not look at. Paradoxically, these two apparently opposing qualities in Freud — the remorseless search for the other, the object, the thing outside himself — and the injection into that of his own insurmountable fears, are what provides his work with its almost terrifying tension and strain..."

In 1975, Freud painted one of his closest friends, and the contemporary artist besides Bacon he admired: Frank Auerbach, a stunningly handsome man Freud and Bacon had first met in a Soho club. Freud depicted his friend looking down, his forehead a sculptural study in concentration. "Lucian Freud has put more of the human forehead into pictures than you can gather in the whole history of painting," Gowing later wrote. After sitting for a number of three-hour sessions, Auerbach would later observe of Freud's intense scrutiny: "I think of Lucian's attention to his subject. If his concentrated interest were to falter, he would come off the tightrope. He has no safety net of manner."

In 1976, the American artist R. B. Kitaj, who lived in London and taught at the Slade School throughout the 1960s, organized an exhibit at the Hayward Gallery called *The Human Clay* (a phrase taken from an Auden poem), which represented painters he felt belonged to what he called "the School of London," a term he coined for the show. Sponsored by the Arts Council of Great Britain, it included thirty-five painters, all of whom focused on the human figure. Figuration had regained popularity in the United States, starting with the advent of pop art in the 1960s, and artists like Chuck Close had already insured that the portrait was making a comeback. Alice Neel, famous for her scathing psychological studies — often nude — had her first Whitney retrospective in 1974.

The roster included many of Freud's Colony Room friends: Auerbach, Bacon, and Michael Andrews, as well as David Hockney, Leon Kossoff, Henry Moore (an artist whose sentimentality Freud detested), and Kitaj himself. As he wrote in an introduction to the exhibit: "Don't listen to the fools who say either that pictures of people can be of no consequence or that painting is finished. There is much to be done.... The bottom line is that there are artistic personalities in this small island more unique and strong and I think numerous than anywhere in the world outside America's jolting artistic vigor.... If some of the strange and fascinating personalities you may encounter here were given a fraction of the internationalist attention and encouragement reserved in this barren time for provincial and orthodox vanguardism, a School of London might become even more real than the one I have construed in my head."

Although the artists mostly disavowed the label, the term

School of London stuck (and Freud is still loosely associated with it). But it didn't necessarily convey immediate artistic or financial success to its members. Freud barely scraped by. Annie Freud recalls times that were "very scary" financially. The artist told John Gruen (whom he drove to his Paddington studio in what Gruen identified as a Silver Cloud Rolls Royce), that when Sigmund Freud died, his grandchildren had each inherited an equal portion of his considerable annual royalties. But of course, there was always Freud's compulsive gambling, and the artist acknowledged to Martin Gayford that he went through a long dry patch.

"My pictures weren't selling. I had a dealer but they neither sold my things nor exhibited them. Suddenly I found I had no income." Freud's last show at Marlborough had been in 1968; he left the gallery in 1972 and was represented by Anthony d'Offay and James Kirkman (who had been at Marlborough) for the next decade, after which Kirkman represented him alone until 1992.

According to Kirkman, "The Sigmund Freud estate royalties were very modest. Lucian lived in an apartment that most people would call a hovel. When he had a Rolls or Bentley it was always beaten-up and second hand. When you were selling his work, there weren't a lot of books or catalogs to push around. All Lucian's paintings were difficult to sell. His paintings would sell for about 1,000 pounds and he produced maybe half a dozen paintings a year. Because of his gambling, he was always in urgent need of money."

Gruen was surprised to see Freud's modest studio, in a run-down building with no address and no name on the doorbell. "Two small rooms, each containing a single bed, an easel, a painting table and one or two chairs." Freud explained that one room was for daytime paintings and one for nighttime. As someone who required very little sleep, Freud had been painting at night for years; over time he had developed a regimented day-night work pattern that would reach its apogee at his next studio, in Holland Park, and that he kept up nearly until the day of his death. He was quite proud of having neither a street address nor a telephone. If anyone wanted to reach him, they had to either just appear or send a telegram; even his children sent telegrams.

As his various children got older, Freud had developed more of a relationship with them, at least some of them. Between the mid-seventies through the mid-eighties, he regularly painted his daughters, Annie, Annabel, Rose, Bella, Esther, Susie, and Ib, both dressed and nude. And in two cases, both pregnant and nude; his pregnant eldest daughter, Annie, is depicted naked in *Annie and Alice* (1975) and a full, frontal, pregnant nude Annabel appears in *Naked Portrait II* (1980–81). He also painted his son Ali. Unlike most of his other portraits, those of his children were (usually) named.

"I paint only the people who are close to me. And who closer than my children? If I thought it odd to paint them, I would never have done so," Freud explained to John Richardson. "For me, painting people naked, regardless of whether they are lovers, children or friends, is never an erotic situation. The sitter and I are involved in making a painting, not love. These are things that people who are not painters fail to understand. Besides, there's something about a person being naked in front of you that invokes consideration — you could even call it chivalry — on my part; in the case of my children, a father's consideration as well as a painter's. They make it all right to paint them. I don't feel I'm under pressure from them."

Still, the situation remains an anomaly (although there are some examples in photography, such as Sally Mann, who photographed her children nude). Freud may be the only painter besides Alice Neel, who painted her daughter-in-law, Nancy, pregnant in 1963, to do so. As Freud told Leigh Bowery in a 1991 interview, "My naked daughters have nothing to be ashamed of."

Although Freud said that the painter-model relationship was not an erotic one, that was certainly not the case with most of his female models, many of whom also became his lovers and, in some instances, the mothers of his children. In fact, Annie points out that there are some portraits that seem to have captured the model just after intercourse, such as "some of those amazing nudes of Jacquetta, and those famous paintings of Penny Cuthbertson that were hugely scandalous. They look like paintings done in-between love making."

Of his working relationship with models, Freud has said, "The painting is always done very much with their cooperation." However, he acknowledged that the stakes were understandably higher when the model posed naked. "The problem with painting a nude, of course, is that it deepens the transaction."

In a lengthy 2009 interview with curator Michael Auping, Freud elaborated. "All portraits are difficult for me. But a nude presents different challenges. When someone is naked, there is in effect nothing to be hidden. You are stripped of your costume, as it were. Not everyone wants to be that honest about themselves. That means I feel an obligation to be equally honest in how I represent their honesty. It's a matter of responsibility. I'm not trying to be a philosopher. I'm more of a realist. I'm just trying to see and understand the people that make up my life. I think of my painting as a continuous group portrait." Painting family members, Freud explained, "is easier because they are more available to me."

Freud's daughters have spoken on-camera about the experience of posing — both naked and not — for their father. It was certainly one way to "get the good bit" of Lucian (as Esther put it in the 2004 documentary) by accepting him for who he was. As Isobel succinctly remarked, "Posing was a way of being in a relationship with my Dad." (Still, as a child, she hated being dragged off "literally screaming and crying from family life on a Sunday, and I didn't want to go" to sit for him.) The filial nudes, like his daughters themselves, have very different auras.

In *Annie and Alice* (1975) Annie (who was also depicted nude at fifteen in *Naked Child Laughing*), is in the foreground, her pregnant belly protruding, her face slightly apprehensive, while a female friend, Alice, sleeps behind her, one hand on Annie's side. The painting has an intimate, rather than erotic feeling, although the relationship between the two women is undefined. "She was a very good friend of Dad's, but more than that I am not going to say. She was both of our friends. It was completely comfortable. Because two girls are naked together, people are 'Oooh, oooh,' but it's just two women without their clothes on lying on the bed, who are friends, and one is pregnant. The rest is all invention."

Annie vividly recalls sitting for *Naked Child Laughing:* "We had loads of fun, and were always laughing. He often lived in places where there were mice and we would listen to them squeak behind the walls and we had lots of nicknames for each other and things. I am interested in the phrase 'deepening the transaction,' and that to me is the issue. Because it is as much to do with power. I'm moving away from the idea of the sexual. I don't mean to say I discount it. But I put it in a context in which personal power for me is the real issue. And that [is] where I feel the truth is. Because I mean I can't speak for other people, but it's not the most natural thing in the world. On the other hand, if he painted other women nude and didn't paint his daughters nude, that would be sort of weird. It's like saying it's okay for some but not for others, and that somehow dirties it." Posing naked did suggest (even if unconsciously) a certain amount of intimacy, she agrees, "although it never, never got mentioned, it was often in my mind."

Still, the experience had its moments of acute discomfort. "To some extent I did have a sort of modesty and anxiety, not because of anything truly improper ever, ever ever, but simply because having your nipples bare and somebody look at them. And I remember one particular time, I brought my hair forward to cover them, and he leant forward with his paintbrush and put my hair behind my shoulder, and that wasn't so easy."

Kitty, Annie's mother, was considerably less accepting. "When my mother found out, probably from me, that I was sitting for this painting without any clothes on, she did write to him and the letter was delivered while I was there. And that was very, very uncomfortable because I didn't want my mother to disapprove. Well you can just imagine. And the letter was sort of critical and saying that she was worried for me and that it wasn't good for me and so on. And my Dad laughed, and said if [Jacob] Epstein [the eminent sculptor who was Kitty's father] could read this, he'd turn over in his grave."

Ib (1977–78) shows Freud's sixteen-year-old daughter by Suzy Boyt, seated on a brown sofa, in a relatively modest pose, with closed legs bent to one side. That is certainly not the case in *Rose* (1978–79), of Ib's older sister, then about nineteen, a much more explicit nude. She's posing with one sharply bent knee clearly exposing her genitalia. It's an earthy, fleshy work, and her discarded shoes under the bed convey a slightly illicit feeling—that she is a mistress rather than a daughter. Yet as with all of Freud's nudes, there is a strong air of detachment.

Rose, who at the time lived around the corner from her father's studio and saw him fairly regularly (both her father and boyfriend helped her with the rent), has said she is very proud of the piece. "I think it's a great painting... I certainly have no regrets whatsoever, and I wouldn't say I would do it again tomorrow—I would do it again tomorrow if I was still nineteen.

It's amazing what went on during that sitting. There was a certain amount of combat possibly under the surface — and maybe some of it more on the surface."

Her uncomfortable position, with her heel jammed up against her thigh, didn't reduce the tension, and Freud has caught her coiled rage. But her pose was a deliberate choice. "I didn't want to feel really sort of floppy and soggy. I wanted to feel I am just about to spring into action, so I was in a position that for me felt a bit guarded and a bit aggressive. I could have been extremely, extremely, extremely angry and I wasn't, and I felt there was a potential for me suddenly to stand up and say, 'Look, fuck off, I'm not sitting anymore, or where were you when I needed you, you bastard?' or something like that. And I think he maybe was a little bit worried in case I was suddenly going to actually spring up and protest. I wouldn't try and pretend that it was simple, what was going on, but the fact of not having any clothes on didn't to me make it any more complicated. If I hadn't been his daughter ... But I was his daughter, and that meant people immediately think, because he was Sigmund Freud's grandson, that we've all got an Oedipal complex. And it seems to me, once someone starts thinking like that, there is no point in talking to them."

Freud more or less dismissed the notion that a father painting his daughter naked might be considered inappropriately intimate. "Painting my daughter was a way of being with her," he said of the portrait of Rose. "She chose to sit in the nude, and she found a pose that allowed her to relax." (This is not exactly Rose's point of view.) "When I become immersed in the process of painting someone, I can lose their relationship to me and just see them as beings, as animals. I'm interested in them as animals in the natural sense, if you know what I mean."

Esther (1980) is a straightforward nude of the yet-to-be-published novelist on a sofa, her head turned rather wistfully to one side. She recalls how the painting came about. "When I went for my first sitting, I went into the studio, and I was aware that there were these huge canvases around me that had paintings of naked women, so I took my clothes off and sat on the sofa. My father once said, 'Oh my daughters had nothing to be ashamed of,' and we didn't. It never occurred to me to be ashamed."

In *Naked Portrait II* (1980–81), Annabel, Freud's second daughter by Kitty, is depicted very pregnant and asleep on a sofa. The painting is unsparing in its detail, from her swollen breasts to the redness above her distended belly; she gave birth the next day. (Martin Filler, in *Vanity Fair,* described it as "a puzzling act of paternal attention.") As Gowing wrote, rather hyperbolically, "The pregnancy, which has run full term, culminates in a ripeness with the veinous bloom of some great fruit . . ."

Freud's clothed portraits of his daughters are rather tender. *Annabel Sleeping* (1978–79) shows her from the back, modestly attired in a pale-blue dressing gown, only her feet bare. She is sleeping on her side, facing a pile of painting rags that look like a foamy wave.

Bella (1980) is a close-up of his daughter asleep in a black dress with an embroidered collar, her lips slightly parted; a 1981 version shows her in the same dress, from a greater distance, her arms crossed on her breast; it has a certain peace about it. "I left home when I was sixteen and moved to London and immediately started sitting for my father, and sat on and off for the next eight years. I had this black dress with flowers embroidered on it and Dad immediately took a liking to it, so he did two pictures in quick succession with that dress. And then, I can't remember when I did my nude, but I think it was after that," she recalled in the Auerbach documentary.

"Always when I used to go and sit however troubled I was, I always felt that I left it at the door, which was a relief, you know it was fantastic as a turbulent teenager just to be able to stop freaking out for a little bit. And then he would make a very nice atmosphere and was very considerate, it was always nice and warm and lots of lovely food or we'd go out. He'd make it nice in a way that was special to each person, so he'd get our maximum cooperation or enjoyment as well."

In the 2012 documentary by Randall Wright, *Lucian Freud: Painted Life,* Bella spoke about posing naked: "I did two paintings first before I did any nudes and then I thought that's what he would like so I tried it out, and then as soon as I started I just felt fine. There was no weird feeling."

Esther (1982–83) shows Esther's head against a pillow, eyes wide open. "It is incredible to me how completely my arm is still my arm. That is exactly the shape of my arm. And I remember being a little bit disappointed by the painting. I wanted to be a great beauty and there I was myself. I did think that I looked like a very large person in the painting and I'm quite a small person. And I said, 'I'm not as big as that' and he said 'that's what you think.' And I always liked that . . . he not trying to depict an image of me. He's painting who I *am.*"

As Gowing has accurately observed, Freud was never in the least concerned by what was or was not considered taboo. Clothed or not, Freud's portraits of his daughters, a self-contained category unto themselves, did, as Robert Hughes wrote, somehow "bypass decorum while preserving respect."

New Views

I N LATE 1977, Freud moved to a new studio, a large, top-floor space in upscale Holland Park, but he kept his studio in Notting Hill. Before moving in, he installed a skylight. "Looking at humans with light streaming down on them is something I terribly liked," he told Feaver. He also installed some foliage, and began the painting *Two Plants* (1977–80), which would become the cover of the first monograph on him, by Lawrence Gowing, published by Thames and Hudson in 1982. "I wanted to have a really biological feeling of things growing up and fading, and leaves coming up and others dying," he said.

Freud also did two unusual paintings featuring male nudes. In the first, *Naked Man with Rat* (1977–78), a long-haired man is lying on a sofa, a rat clutched in one hand. The rat's long, suggestive tail stretches across the man's inner thigh, running intimately close to his genitals and mirroring them, yet looking oddly matter-of-fact. (The rat belonged to a friend, Katy McEwen, who kept Japanese laboratory rats.) "For Freud, the penis and the tail are simply different types of appendages," Michael Auping would later observe in a catalogue for the National Portrait Gallery Freud retrospective in 2012.

It has never been a critics' favorite. "For all the strangeness of his story, we have no interest in the rat-holding man," Charles Darwent wrote in *The Independent:* "Indeed, that we are forbidden to be interested in him. For all the information we are given — too much, in the case of his genitals — we know nothing about the man with the rat, and can only know nothing. Is this portraiture? I have my doubts. Perhaps it is more useful to think of Freud as a painter of still lifes (or, more appositely, natures mortes) who happens to work with human flesh rather than apples or pears."

The same man is shown naked in a second portrait, begun in 1978 but completed in 1980, with his lover, in pajamas. Their pose is remarkably relaxed; the younger, naked man's bent left knee rests comfortably against the left leg of his older lover, which is stretched across the younger's right thigh. Their eyes are closed. The meshing of their legs, and the younger man's hand on the older man's ankle, are palpably tender. There is nothing salacious about the work; it is about a longtime couple still deeply in love.

Freud himself had just entered a new romance. His relationship with Jacquetta Eliot, which had gone on for several years, had just recently unravelled. During their time together, he had done a number of strong nudes of her, including *Small Naked Portrait* (1975). The end of the relationship was signaled in his final painting of her, *Last Portrait* (1976–77); in it she is modestly clothed.

Eliot, who as Freud's oldest daughter Annie put it, was one of "many, many, many, many, many" titled ladies that Freud was involved with over the years, later recalled the artist as "electric, and everything about him was electric. Just the way he walked into the room and the way he breathed. He breathed like an animal that's excited. And he was very animal and feral, and he did exactly what he wanted." His appeal was manifold: Freud was "funny and clever, ardent, urgent and fantastically intimate," and she also alluded to the pleasures of the studio, which included drinking "champagne on dirty floorboards."

Jacquetta had frequently found posing a welcome refuge

from what was going on in her married life at home, but as time went on their sessions became increasingly tense. "Sometimes I resented it terribly, sometimes I was so glad to get away from the domestic life and be able to go there and relax, and embark on something that made total sense to me. And then sometimes . . . I wanted to jack it in and leave the room, and it was always quite difficult. We gave up on several paintings because it just became so difficult. We were crashing around at that time. There was [*sic*] a lot of books flying around the room. It was during one of our many breakups." Eventually the difficulties outweighed the rewards.

John Richardson offers an interesting theory about Freud's many titled mistresses: "I think he had to reinvent himself as an Englishman and he wanted to reinvent himself as an Englishman of some social stature. And I think he loved the traditional English way of life, he loved country-house life, and he fitted in superbly well to that. I don't think it was ordinary snobbery.

"I mean he also I think he took advantage of the fact that the sort of English upper-class men or English aristocrats tend to make lousy husbands, I mean they are unfaithful, drunken, much more interested in sort of masculine sports and life. And the 'little woman' — quote unquote — has a lousy time. And I think that Lucian took advantage of this situation. And here was this very attractive sexy enormously gifted sort of fascinating and mysterious painter who comes into their lives and they fell like a ton of bricks."

As Annie Freud puts it, "I think to a degree my father did like the idea of being a kind of Scarlet Pimpernel, this mysterious man that no woman can resist . . . who paints naked girls."

Freud was also excited by "extreme wealth," she says. "I remember once he had an incredibly rich girlfriend and she bought him a jar of caviar and he ate it with a spoon. And he said, 'It's the weirdest feeling putting a spoonful of food into my mouth that is worth a thousand pounds.' He loved that sort of wild excess."

Freud had always moved at whim through the strata of English society. His lifestyle ranged from Paddington's poorest neighborhoods to England's greatest houses. And he was notorious for choosing friends and lovers from both the upper and lower classes. As Martin Filler observed in *Vanity Fair,* "Freud has had a definite class system of women in his life, strong aristocrats and feckless waifs." To that he might well have added beautiful art students. Freud's next romance was with a young woman younger than several of his daughters named Celia Paul. She was just eighteen when Freud first discovered her in 1977 at the Slade School of Art.

Paul recalls the moment wistfully in the Auerbach documentary, creating an image so romantic it is almost a cliché. "He came into the life drawing studio, very intense, and gave a very intense stare at the model who was lying on the floor, and he was wearing this beautiful grey suit and sort of pale shirt, and smoking a French cigarette and just very, very charismatic." Despite his powerful presence, Paul got up the nerve to ask him to see her work. Freud was nothing if not candid. "He told me afterwards that he'd come to Slade to find a girl, and that girl was me. So I think he'd very much come to Slade to find someone."

Freud took her back to his studio and showed her a painting, *Two Plants.* "I think he would have liked to seduce me there and then, but that didn't happen. I'd been brought up in a religious family, I'd never had a sexual thing with a boy at all. I was really quite disturbed by his predatoriness."

Freud and Paul did not immediately become lovers. Nor did he paint her until several years after they became involved. "I remember I sat for *Naked Girl with Egg* [1980–81]. I was so very unhappy about it. It felt very like me. I was sort of excruciated by how like it was. I think it's a very pitiless painting . . . I know

I used to cry a lot and actually he was very nice about it, but his work is all about truth. And the only way to tell the truth is by concentrating and not turning away from it ... I was quite a shy young woman, and it did feel very exposing, to lie there and he stood very close to me and kind of scrutinized me in a way that made me feel very undesirable, felt quite clinical, almost as though I was on a surgical bed." It's an extraordinary work, with Paul, whose waiflike blonde beauty is somewhat reminiscent of Caroline Blackwood's, lying back on a dark bed, her face delicate and small-featured; her large breasts falling to one side, her legs curled beneath her. Coyly placed on the edge of a round table near her right knee is a small pan with a hardboiled egg sliced in half, its twin yolks echoing her nipples.

Their relationship was consummated a few months later, but Paul always knew that Freud was not monogamous. Still, the relationship continued until the late 1980s. In 1985, when Freud painted *Girl in a Striped Nightshirt,* Paul was pregnant with their son, Frank, the youngest of Freud's children. "I suppose I love the one of me in the striped night shirt, partly because I was pregnant at the time and so it's a sort of a record of our closeness and I think you can sort of see that he loves me in it. And there seems to be something so tender about it," Paul says of the painting. "At that time Lucian and I were very close and my mother was completely grief-stricken over the loss of my father. I wanted the baby for her, to give her someone to go on living for. But it was also because I loved Lucian so much and he loved me, and he wanted us to have a baby."

Although Paul left the infant with her mother in Cambridge just weeks after his birth, Freud apparently felt that Celia had distanced herself. There's a very different feeling in *Painter and Model,* done in 1986–87. Quite unlike anything else Freud has painted, it shows Celia Paul in a paint-spattered dress, her hands purposefully clasping a phallic brush, one bare foot crushing a tube from which paint oozes. In front of her sprawls a naked man on a brown leather couch, his genitals fully exposed to her female gaze; a total role reversal.

She speaks about it proudly in the Randall Wright documentary. "I'm the painter and I'm standing in a position of power really, and one thing that's interesting to me is it's the last painting he did of me. I'd become myself more ambitious as a painter and I was preparing for my first solo exhibition in London and I had also a few years before given birth to our son Frank, and I think Lucian's feelings about me in this painting are quite ambivalent. I'm holding a very definitely angled brush and standing on a tube of paint which is oozing. The brush and the oozing paint I feel are kind of sexual symbols. And I think suddenly my becoming both the lover and a seriously ambitious painter put me in a different position and I was no longer kind of the voluptuous figure lying on the bed . . . "

As John Richardson bluntly put it in that same documentary, "For Lucian I think that painting was akin to fucking. I think that his creativeness, I should have said, was very akin to fucking. The sex act and the intellectual act or whatever you call it of painting, were in some ways interchangeable. I think that he had no difficulty transforming sexual notions into paint and paint into sexual notions. I think the two aspects of his senses came together in the act of painting."

The Way of All Flesh

I N 1981, FREUD was included in a show called *A New Spirit in Painting* at the Royal Academy, which cast Freud, Bacon, Kitaj, and Auerbach, among others, as founders of a new school of figuration. That October, he had a show at the Anthony d'Offay gallery, *Lucian Freud,* which included twenty-one works.

In 1982, Thames and Hudson published Lawrence Gowing's monograph on Freud. In addition to the standard print run, it was also brought out in a deluxe edition of one hundred copies, in editions of twenty-five, each including one of four original etchings. It posited Freud as a modern master, tracing his artistic trajectory from childhood on. According to James Kirkman, the monograph imbued Freud's art with a new level of credibility. "Gowing's book was very perceptive and beautifully produced," he says. "It was the first real book on his work."

Partly spurred by wanting to include etchings in the new book, Freud had returned to the form for the first time in over three decades. He produced fifteen etchings in 1982, including two of his monographer, Gowing, and he would continue to make etchings for the rest of his career. Freud's skill as a draughtsman is on full display in his etchings, which convey a warmth often lacking in his paintings.

In 1981–82, Freud, who never lacked for friends in high

places, and as usual, needed money, did a commissioned portrait of Baron Thyssen. Flanked by two security guards, the baron mounted the six flights to Freud's Holland Park studio. Freud had tacked a photograph of a prize painting from the Baron's famous collection (the Thyssen-Bornemisza collection), Watteau's *Pierrot Content,* to the wall behind him. The reference, to the amorous jealousy of the commedia dell'arte character Pierrot (Baron Thyssen was known as a consummate playboy), was probably not lost on the baron — and it was not lost on critics.

Portrait of a Man (1981–82) is a close-up of the baron's imposing head and shoulders, his face juxtaposed against the image of Pierrot with a woman playing a mandolin. (Freud would later do a second, full-figure portrait of Baron Thyssen [*Man in a Chair,* 1983–85], showing him with his hands splayed on his thighs, a pile of studio rags by his side.)

Over the next year, the Watteau image itself would move from the background of a canvas to its foreground as the subject of Freud's next major opus: *Large Interior WII (After Watteau).* It is loosely based on the Watteau work, but instead of using commedia dell'arte characters, Freud has grouped his real-life intimates: two lovers and two children; Celia Paul, Bella, Suzy Boyt, and her son Kai, whom Freud considered a stepson. A fifth child, Star, was, as Freud put it, on loan.

The studio setting is plainly exposed — the real drama behind the posed and costumed drama — including a sink which, for some sittings, had a deliberately running tap to emulate a fountain. While highly regarded by many critics, it was not universally admired when it was first shown in 1983. One critic, who decried the "sordid room" and "nasty sink" depicted in the painting, wrote: "Lucian Freud has always seemed to me grossly overrated and this picture confirms my opinion."

The most artificial and "posed" of all Freud's work, it seems an attempt by Freud, who was obsessive about "keeping every relationship and every strand of his life so very separate," as Celia Paul put it, to gather together some of those variant threads; to create a synthesized family on canvas, self-consciously framed in art-historical terms, with his studio serving as a sort of proscenium. Nothing about it is real, including the fact that most of the sitters posed separately or in twos after the initial sketch. Freud himself described it as "the nearest thing I've come to casting people, rather than painting them. But they are still portraits, really: people and to what degree they are affected by being near each other."

But the sitters felt — and were — distinctly separate. Bella recalled in the 2012 documentary: "That was a really hard picture to sit for, because it was so uncomfortable sitting upright holding this horrible mandolin and wearing this really uncomfortable dress that had gold thread in it, which was rather prickly. And also when we were all together, all the heat from the different bodies was really uncomfortable. But then after he'd sketched it in and put us in place, we'd probably be two at a time and sometimes alone."

The work is a dramatic departure from the artist's usual modus operandi. As Celia Paul put it, "When he was with a person, nobody else mattered to him. And I think he was challenged to do a painting with a lot of people that mattered to him in his life altogether. But the interesting thing in that painting is that I only ever sat with Bella. I never sat with any of the other figures in the painting. So I think it gives it kind of quite a melancholy feeling . . . all the individuals are sort of isolated in their own inner space."

"The link is me, I'm the connection," Freud told Feaver, who calls the painting "Freud's great studio painting," an artistic feat in the late-twentieth century. "The reason it comes off so brilliantly is the different nervous feelings of the sitters. The whole painting has a feeling of people not quite getting on, but all part of a circle. And of course the focus of the whole painting is Lucian himself. They're there because of Lucian."

Freud's reputation grew exponentially in the mid-to-late 1980s, partly because of a return to interest in figurative painting both in Europe and in America, but also because Freud himself was operating on a larger stage. Says d'Offay: "It wasn't a little club anymore around Lucian. He could be seen as a great British artist, and he made work to sell to museums and to collectors."

As Kirkman put it in the 2012 documentary: "Lucian's painting and his ambitions grew in the '80s, and I think that things were for once beginning to go slightly well for him. He had a nice studio, he was beginning to know some success, he was financially already exceedingly well off. I think that possibly he was becoming slightly more genial ... and he certainly became more productive." Up until then, because of his time-consuming painting process, Freud produced only a few pictures a year, and according to Kirkman was lucky if they sold for 1,000 pounds each. And because he was perpetually short of money, he didn't consign his paintings to his dealer: he insisted they all be bought outright, an unusual and expensive venture for any dealer or gallery.

In 1985, Freud was made a Companion of Honor, an award he accepted, although he turned down a Commander of the Order of the British Empire (CBE) in 1977, which Bacon had also turned down. In 1986, the National Gallery asked him to curate a show from their collections called *The Artist's Eye*. He included twenty-five works by Hals, Velazquez, Chardin, Seurat, Ingres, Cézanne, Vuillard, Degas, Daumier, Whistler, Constable, and Rembrandt. The show ran from June 17 to August 16, 1987. "What do I ask of a painting? I ask it to astonish, disturb, seduce, convince. One quality these paintings share is that they all make me want to go back to work," Freud memorably said in the catalogue. Two Freud paintings were also included, both from 1985–86: *The Painter's Brother Stephen* and *Double Portrait.*

In 1987, a major Freud traveling retrospective organized by the British Arts Council, which included 139 works, from the 1940s to his most recent paintings, opened at the Hirshhorn Museum in Washington. It ran from September 15 to November 29, before traveling to Berlin, Paris, and finally to the Hayward Gallery in London. (Freud was one of the few British artists to have had two retrospectives there; the other artist was Francis Bacon.) Robert Hughes wrote the catalogue essay, still considered a seminal art-historical analysis of the artist. In it, Hughes famously called Freud "the greatest living realist painter." Certainly the show marked a significant turning point in his career. In *The Independent,* Andrew Graham-Dixon wrote of the retrospective when it arrived at the Hayward, where it was on view from February 4 to April 17, "[it] is not just another art exhibition, it is presented as a milestone in cultural history."

The centerpiece of the Hayward show was Freud's female nudes, which had a room of their own. Graham-Dixon called them his "undoubted masterpieces," going on to write:

> ... the bourgeois liberal knee-jerk response to these pictures might result in the view that they are the work of a closet sadist, misogynistically revelling in the indiginities of a genitally exposed, splay-legged womankind.... His female nudes are his greatest paintings, not because they are masterpieces of "realism" (although they are, masterfully, alive to the tiniest differences in the forms of those who sit to him) still less because they embody a kind of fine art of sadism. Painted with immense, wise sympathy, they embody his vision of humanity. Operating as analogies for his glum, lonely sense of himself and others, they are self-revelatory. They are, in a sense, self-portraits.

Lucian Freud with his grandfather, Sigmund, in London, circa 1938

Lucian Freud, circa 1950s, photographed by Walker Evans

Lorna Wishart and Lucian Freud, circa 1945, photographed by Francis Goodman

*Caroline Blackwood, circa 1950s,
photographed by Walker Evans*

Hotel Bedroom, *1954*

Girl with a Kitten, *1947*

Kitty Freud with Annie, circa 1948

Francis Bacon and Lucian Freud, 1974, photographed by Harry Diamond

Lucian Freud with his mother, Lucie, circa 1980, photographed by David Montgomery

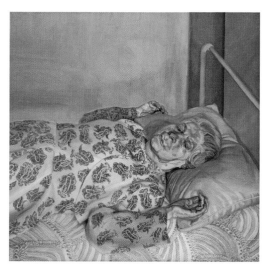

The Painter's Mother Resting I, *1975–76*

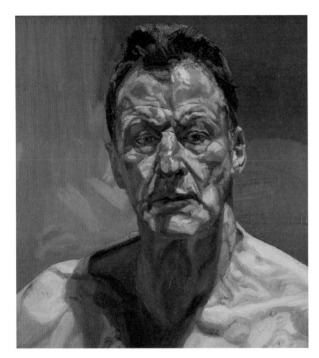

Reflection
(Self-Portrait), *1985*

Working at Night, *2005 , photographed by David Dawson*

Still, according to Kirkman, who helped organize the retrospective, "The Gowing book and the second Hayward show changed things in the UK, but not much in Europe. Freud wasn't famous or feted. He didn't get VIP treatment. The Hirshhorn show was the first time Freud really got publicly well-accepted in North America." As John Russell put it, "[Freud] has never had, nor sought, a large constituency either in this country or anywhere else ... in England he has been unmistakably there, as a disquieting and often worrisome presence.... But he was a leaver, not a joiner, and neither then nor since has he ever fitted into British patterns of life."

The Hirshhorn show was a bonafide blockbuster. It was America's first real introduction to the artist, who had had only one previous show in New York, nearly a decade earlier, an Anthony d'Offay exhibit that traveled to Davis & Long Company, in April 1978. Freud's in-your-face painting style resonated powerfully with a contemporary audience that enthusiastically embraced the 1980s aesthetic: a celebrated return to figuration, painting itself, and neo-expressionism.

Although Freud, who hated being labeled "expressionist," might have had little in common with Julian Schnabel, Jean-Michel Basquiat, David Salle, or even Eric Fischl (the closest to a kindred spirit in terms of style and subject matter), he was clearly obsessed with both figuration and with paint itself, at a time when paint was the medium of the moment, and figurative art ruled. "Art is once again a medium of dreams and memories, of symbols and scenarios," wrote Hilton Kramer, the long-time art critic of the *New York Times:* "It has reacquired its capacity for drama."

James Demetrion, Hirshhorn's director at the time, was widely lauded for his decision not only to take a show that other U.S. venues were reluctant to touch, but to later convince his institution to purchase several major Freuds, including a portrait of performance artist Leigh Bowery, *Nude with Leg Up* (1992). As Demetrion recalls, "I got a call from the British Arts Council saying they had not been able to get it into other museums in the States. Apparently Freud was not well-known outside of Britain, which kind of baffled me. It was odd no New York museum was interested. I just think that his particular way of painting, really zooming in on people, is quite unique. I find it pretty amazing, frankly. There's this kind of unflinching realism. If there were a movement called 'Unflinching Realism,' he would be head of it."

Reviewing the Hirshhorn show in the *New York Times,* John Russell wrote, "We may come out convinced not so much as Mr. Hughes suggests, that Freud is the greatest living realist painter, but rather that he is the *only* living realist painter, and the one who has given back to realism an element of risk and revelation that had long been forfeited.... Anyone who cares about painting would be crazy to miss it."

The exhibit even occasioned a feature-length profile in the *New York Times Sunday Magazine.* "Lucian Freud has become a figure of popular myth, an artist poised between the underworld and the aristocracy and a kind of slumming Faust who prowls lowlife pubs and eats woodcock for breakfast," the piece, by Marina Warner began, making one understand why Freud rarely gave interviews. "In Britain, Lucian Freud's name appears on any connoisseur's list of the country's greatest twentieth-century artists, along with Stanley Spencer and Henry Moore and Francis Bacon; abroad, he is only selectively admired.... Freud's work is easy to admire, difficult to like ... Lucian Freud might have been invented by a modern Musil or Proust: he is, both the man and the artist, a defining antihero of our own fin de siècle."

The Holland Park studio was Freud's first really substantial working space, and he made full use of it, from its broad floorboards and faded, peeling walls — one encrusted with painting rags — to its light-filled windows with their view of rooftops, all of which increasingly appeared in his paintings.

From the time that Freud had gotten the space, he had begun adding strips of canvases to enlarge paintings as he worked on them, literally expanding his artistic vision in real time. The room was sparsely furnished, with bare ceiling lights, a brown Chesterfield couch spewing stuffing, and various brass and iron bedsteads. (The bursting sofa is used to great effect in *Painter and Model,* 1986–87, holding a splayed male nude, and *Bella and Esther,* 1987–88, a double-portrait of his snugly ensconced daughters.)

His stiff, stained painting rags served as an ever more pronounced prop. In 1987–89 Freud painted a recent model, Sophie de Stempel, nude, standing upright against a virtual wall of paint rags, an image that is an odd spin on the standard nude against bed linen. In *Standing by the Rags,* the oyster hue of the rags creates a contrast with the flesh tones of her skin, forming a rich, foamy-looking backdrop. Freud did a similar painting the following year, *Lying by the Rags,* in which the same model is stretched out on the bare floorboards, a border of rags behind her.

In the 2012 documentary, de Stempel recalls: "Lucian always had to challenge himself. He always had to push himself further, and as he got older he started doing more and more ambitious paintings. He was in his late sixties when he did the two 'By the Rags.' I think this was a sort of test on [*sic*] himself. It was a test on his concentration and a test on his memory."

De Stempel had sought Freud out to paint her after she heard the parents of some friends calling Lucian "'a disgusting filthy Jew.' I remember them saying this and I remember thinking, 'Oh, I wonder if I could meet him . . . ' He was demanding so much commitment, so much time that you really couldn't not love someone to be in that situation. You had to love them a bit, because they are trying to create out of nothing, this magic creation from nothing, from a blank canvas and there is an enormous amount of crisis going into that. He would jump up and down and scream. It was really hard for him to bring it about. He was working in this immense intensity. This was year in, year out, this was Christmas Day, New Year's, there was never a day off. . . . He had this extraordinary energy and he was working standing up for seven, eight hours through the night. And then he would be up at seven painting someone else, which to me seemed incredible."

Freud's rags also played a major role in *Two Men in the Studio* (1987–89), a take-off on another commedia dell'arte painting by Watteau, *Gilles*. Angus Cook, a poet and writer, stands on a bed, naked, his crossed arms over his head. Behind him, on an easel, *Standing by the Rags* can be seen, a direct reference to the rag-pile by his right side. From beneath the bed, two feet emerge, belonging to Cook's friend, the artist Cerith Wyn Evans.

As Cook later aptly wrote in a catalogue essay for a Matthew Marks show in 1993: "The rags were his cutting room floor. Doubly discarded, they were past their best as bed sheets and too stained to be used anymore to wipe his brushes. The rags and the paint on them, the outtakes of previous paintings, are, by becoming his subjects, restored. There is a magnanimity to them. They have a reciprocity with the human figure and have, for all their specificity, an emergent quality. Lucian has mentioned their 'watery and wavy aspect.'"

In 1989, Freud's mother died. Freud did his final image of her the day after her death, a simple charcoal drawing of an expired human head; it looks almost like a mummy portrait.

Annie Freud recalls her father's often fraught relationship with his mother, giving as an example a visit that abruptly ended when, despite Lucian's many protests, Lucie insisted on fetching and showing him a pot made by Lucie Rie, an artist she collected, whom he detested. But at the same time, she adds, "He was in some ways extremely tender towards her. I remember one night ... I think we'd had dinner with my grandmother. And [Dad] said something to her, and she said [colloquially], 'Oh I'm not in the picture,' meaning, 'I don't understand.' And he said, 'You're in all the pictures.'"

In 1990, Lucian Freud found his next great subject, an over-the-top Australian performance artist named Leigh Bowery, whom Freud first met at the Anthony d'Offay Gallery, where Bowery had done a week-long installation piece starring himself in an array of exotic getups a few years earlier. Wyn Evans and Cook arranged a meeting between the artist and the flamboyantly dressed performer (sequins were a favorite motif) at Harry's Bar, because they wanted to "get one back on Lucian ... all those sequins. We thought we'd get Lucian to put that old beige paint away."

Freud had seen Bowery around before and been impressed by his monolithic legs. A massive man capable of extraordinary physical flexibility, Bowery had the big bald head of a Buddha. Using Bowery as a model over the next four years, until his death from AIDS on December 31, 1994, Freud produced some of the most astonishing work of his career, paintings monumental in both their scale and sensibility.

Freud once said that sculpture was his first love, and he owned a copy of Rodin's *Balzac,* which occupied a place of honor at the head of the Holland Park stairs, guarding the studio entrance. Bowery's form naturally lent itself to a sculptural approach, and Freud energetically exploited the potential of both his huge figure and his ability to maintain contorted poses. The two were highly attuned to each other. As a performance artist, Bowery, who had many body piercings, was usually turned out in full regalia, from quirky clothes to jewelry. But when he first entered Freud's studio, he simply stripped and removed all his studs, without Freud's bidding. He wore no makeup, and he shaved himself from head to foot, to afford the artist even fuller exposure.

In the first portrait, *Leigh Bowery (Seated)* (1990), his figure overwhelms a red armchair. Indeed, Freud kept enlarging the canvas with new strips in order to contain him. And yet, as large as he was, Bowery had an almost dancerly grace. Even in a seemingly straightforward pose like that of *Naked Man, Back View* (1991–92), where only the model's back is shown as he sits on a low ottoman, Freud managed to capture a sense of both the baroque and the Buddha-like embedded in Bowery's presence.

He was inspired both by Bowery's "wonderfully buoyant bulk" and "the quality of his mind." Freud described Bowery as "very aware, very relaxed, and very encouraging in the way that physical presence can be. His feelings about clothes extend to his physiognomy even, so that the way he edits his body is amazingly aware and amazingly abandoned."

Nude with Leg Up, painted in 1992, shows Bowery reclining on the studio floorboards, amidst a sea of Freud's painting rags, one leg improbably propped up on a green-striped mattress. For once he looks life-size rather than larger than life, since Freud has him anchor the center of the composition, which is made up of the mattress, the rags, the floorboards and the bottom of a window. In *Leigh under the Skylight* (1994), the model is standing on a covered table, his head poking up towards the ceiling. Although his ankles are delicately crossed, his huge body is torqued in a pose that recalls Rodin.

Freud also painted Bowery lying naked on a bed with Nicola Bateman, who worked with him and married him not long before his death. *And the Bridegroom* (1993) is a painterly performance piece, a theatrical composition rendered in a hushed palette that heightens the drama. A bed, heavily draped in a beige sheet, sits in front of a black folding screen. The background of the painting consists simply of brown floorboards and yellowish walls. Bowery and Bateman, both nude, lie in state on the bed, sculptures on a pedestal, their heads turned away from each other. Bateman, a thin but rounded figure, has one slender ankle draped over Bowery's thick thigh; her long hair flows off the edge of the bed. Named after a line in an A. E. Housman poem (although Bowery wanted Freud to call it "A Fag and his Hag"), it's a one-act tour de force. "I've always been interested in bringing a certain kind of drama to portraiture," Freud said, "the kind of drama that I found in paintings of the past. If a painting doesn't have drama, it doesn't work; it's just paint out of the tube."

Nicola Bateman appears in several other paintings, including a poignant footnote to Bowery's death, the strange piece *Girl Sitting in the Attic Doorway* (1995), which shows the naked Bateman perched in an alcove above a wardrobe. "As he was coming towards the end of painting . . . it was around that time that Leigh started to die. . . . And I would sit up there. And I spent the whole time just thinking about Leigh . . . and that he's dying right now. I think it gave me a little bit of breathing space from the situation." When Bowery died, Freud had his body flown back to Australia.

For his part, Bowery had contributed to the existing Freud literature a year or so earlier, with a sharp and revealing interview for a magazine called *Lovely Jobly,* which was later reprinted in the Matthew Marks catalogue for the 1993 show *Freud, Recent Drawings and Etchings.* In the interview, Bowery asked Freud why he thought he was sometimes called a misogynist. Freud responded, "One of the classical instincts of the human idiot is to take a single bone and to reconstruct the whole animal from it . . . I think the idea of misogyny is a stimulant to feminists, and it's rather like anti-Semites looking for Jewish noses everywhere." Asked if he had any "feminist fans," Freud replied, "My daughter Esther, or doesn't that count? Also I'm a feminist but I'm not sure to what degree I'm my fan."

Bowery commented that Freud often worked from his lovers. "Yes, but you can't do two things at once," was Freud's quick retort. "When did you get the idea of working from your naked grownup daughters?" Bowery asked. "When I started painting naked people," Freud said. "I can't think of another artist who had done that. It must make things, well, slightly extreme," Bowery continued. "My naked daughters have nothing to be ashamed of," Freud famously insisted. "But how would you feel being naked in front of them?" "I wouldn't be naked in front of them in case they thought I was a nudist."

Bowery left another legacy: about a year before he died he had introduced Freud to another larger-than-life model, Sue Tilley, who would become one of the artist's most famous — and highest-priced — subjects. Tilley worked as a Benefits Supervisor at the West End Job Centre in Charing Cross. Bowery had wanted the two to meet, partly, he told Tilley, because sitting for Freud was like "getting a university education."

Tilley recalled her first encounter with Lucian, at a Soho nightclub, where he told her that her lipstick was too blue. He later took her to lunch, "and gave me a full inspection, stared at me and everything and then just asked me to model." Before she went to sit for the artist the first time, Bowery made her practice by "stripping off on my settee at home."

"When you went to his house to model, you couldn't wear any makeup, you weren't allowed," she recalls. Freud noticed every tiny nuance, from the merest smudge of eye makeup (Tilley was rushed off to the bathroom to remove it) to an incidental change of shampoo that slightly altered her hair color. "I had to be there at seven in the morning, and each painting took about nine months. I'd sit about two or three times a week, including on the weekends, for about six or seven hours," she says. She got twenty pounds a day to pose.

Tilley describes Freud as "entertaining, but you know those people that have a personality that's all over the place, you couldn't call him. He'd be a bit quiet, then as loud as could be or he'd be down, or up. He was mean, he was generous, everything, all combined. He was never predictable."

One of the perks of the job was having lunch with Lucian at the River Café. "He was hilarious. I mean, I'm nosy. He was ten times worse. I tried to be subtle at staring at people. There was no subtlety with him. He'd just literally stare right at people he liked the look of, and then say really rude things about them really loud. Knew about tons of things. Very chatty."

Tilley calls the first painting he did of her, *Evening in the Studio* (1993), "the most repulsive thing. I can't even bear to look at it. Because it's horrible." She soon got used to posing nude, thinking, "He's just like a doctor. He's seen plenty of naked people." The image started out with Tilley lying on the floor in an extremely unflattering, awkward position, like, she says, "a big fat crab." Her mottled flesh mimics the mottled walls. Just behind her, Nicola Bateman sits in a chair, embroidering a large piece of fabric that trails down her lap (a former textiles student, she regularly sewed and embellished clothes for Bowery), while Bowery and a dog recline on a bed. Bowery was later erased from the painting because he went to Scotland and was unavailable to pose; Bateman, Tilley, and Pluto, Freud's beloved whippet, remain.

In a second, kinder image, *Benefits Supervisor Resting* (1994), Tilley sits at one end of a couch, her head, small in comparison to her body, tilted back, her neck arched. The third image, *Benefits Supervisor Sleeping* (1995) (which sold for $33.6 million in 2008, at the time the highest price ever for a living artist), shows her curled on the same sofa, one hand cupping a large, flabby breast, one arm flung over the back of the couch; the diametric opposite of a classic odalisque. *Sleeping by the Lion Carpet,* the fourth and final Tilley portrait, is the tamest of these large canvases, depicting Big Sue, as she came to be known, asleep in a leather chair too small for her, a tacky flea-market find, a tapestry with two lions on it, in the background.

If Freud's intention was to "astonish and disturb," as he had said any great painting should, he more than achieved that with his portraits of Tilley. Freud himself remarked that she was "quite feminine in her way," but although she is not treated as a circus freak, her gross obesity is on full display, and she has none of the muscle tone that made Bowery's body look splendidly statuesque rather than crudely heavy or grotesque. There's an almost vaudevillian quality to Freud's Big Sue pieces, as if they are a kind of stunt.

As Freud explained to Feaver (while referring to Velázquez and his images of clowns and dwarfs), "I have perhaps a predilection towards people of unusual or strange proportions, which I don't want to overindulge." Freud was particularly fascinated by "all kinds of spectacular things to do with her [Sue's] size, like amazing craters and things one's never seen before," and "sores and chafes made by weight and heat.... It's flesh without muscle and it has developed a different kind of texture through being such a weight-bearing thing." A photograph of Tilley posing for *Benefits Supervisor Sleeping* shows her in all her immensity, but with flesh that is smoothly pneumatic, rather than as portrayed by Freud: puffy, corroded, on the verge of decay.

Even faithful Freud aficionados like Bruce Bernard, who photographed Tilley in the studio, and later wrote about the portraits in his authoritative 1996 book, *Lucian Freud,* found the first painting, *Evening in the Studio,* hard to stomach. "During the run of his great exhibition at Whitechapel Art Gallery in 1993, he [Freud] introduced a new painting which many have found repellent, and which is difficult to understand simply as a picture, or as an anecdote or narrative." Still, Bernard concludes that the last two portraits in the Big Sue series "are major contributions to the sum of Western painting of the nude, and may even put the final stop to the classical tradition ..."

Observes Tilley, "I think it's honest and true, what he saw. You know how they say he hated women and all that. I think it's a load of rubbish. He loved them. I hate it when people read things into the paintings . . . I think his paintings were far more about composition than telling a story."

To Tilley, Freud's artistic intention seemed straightforward: "to draw you as well as he could. It's all done to test and challenge and see how well he can paint. It was all about getting the paintings as good as he could."

Painting Against Time

A S FREUD GOT older, rather than slowing down, he seemed, if anything, to speed up. In 1992, on the cusp of seventy, and confronting his own old age, he had begun painting an audacious self-portrait, *Painter Working, Reflection* (1992–93). In it, he is totally nude except for his laceless work boots; one hand holds his paint palette, the other wields a painting knife. An art-historical oddity, his was not the first such heroic self-examination. Freud had probably never seen it, but his naked self-portrait closely echoed a famous portrait by the American artist Alice Neel, who boldly painted herself nude at the age of 80, shorn of everything but her glasses, a paint rag, and a brush.

Although throughout his career Freud had consistently painted self-portraits, this was the first time he had stripped himself bare. "Now the very least I can do is paint myself naked," he told Feaver. "It's more difficult than painting people, I find," he said of self-portraits. "Increasingly so. The psychological element is more difficult. I put all sort of expressions in and obscure them."

The artist regarded himself with a typically pitiless gaze. In the finished portrait, Freud looks slightly resigned but certainly not defeated by the indignities of age. He is in admirable shape at seventy-one, with little or no fat on his body, displayed in stark relief against the bare studio walls and floor, a vulnerable but commanding presence on an empty stage. Freud told Feaver that as he worked on the image of his own face, which at first "turned out to be my father," he recalled the haunting theme song from the movie *High Noon,* "I do not know what fate awaits me . . . I only know I must be brave . . . and I must face the man who hates me . . . Or lie a coward . . . in my grave . . ."

In 1991–92 Freud did another image, repeated in 1993, that in its own way is also a self-portrait, or at least a primary key to Freud as a portrait painter. *Still Life with Book* shows his most beloved tome, *Geschichte Aegyptens,* open to two photographs of Egyptian plaster portrait heads from the time of Akhenaten (fourteenth century BC) — similar to those in Sigmund Freud's study that had quite possibly (consciously or not) first kindled the artist's lifelong passion for portraiture. "By painting them I didn't have to go very far afield. I thought about those people a lot. There's nothing like them: they're human before Egyptian in a way," he said. Their faces were, for Freud, more than a moving metaphor — they were a lifelong touchstone.

In both paintings, the book is nestled against a pillow. In the first, the pillow serves as a sort of bookmark, keeping the volume open at another place; in the second, the book rests against what Bruce Bernard calls a "suggestive" pillow, which does indeed look like female genitalia. Freud made another image, *The Eygptian Book,* an etching, in 1994. It also figures, as already mentioned, in one of his famous portraits of his mother.

Julia Auerbach photographed Freud with *Geschichte Aegyptens* in 1989, on the bed on which, a few years later, it was probably painted. In the photo, taken in his studio, framed by paint rags, Freud looks pensively down at it, a pair of glasses (not worn when painting) in his right hand. It was quite literally, his "pillow book," as Feaver put it, "his writer's companion, his Bible . . ."

• • •

Freud's increasingly ambitious works of the last two decades of his life were made possible by his assistant, David Dawson, who started working with Freud in the early 1990s. Amanuensis, model, and trusted friend, Dawson, a painter and photographer, started out working with Freud in the morning, returned home to do his own art, and then went back to Freud's Holland Park studio at dusk, although eventually his job became almost full time. In addition to helping Freud at every stage of a painting, serving as his daily companion, and becoming a frequent model, Dawson also photographed Freud in the studio, producing invaluable and candid images of the reclusive artist at work.

The relationship began in 1989 or 1990 when Dawson first heard that Freud's dealer, James Kirkman, was looking for someone to help work with Freud. Kirkman took him over to Holland Park to meet the artist. "As we started to climb the six flights, Lucian was waiting for us at the top. He was quite small, slim, very light and quick on his feet, and had fantastically bright sparkling eyes," he recalled.

Dawson and Freud met a few times in the kitchen of the Holland Park flat. The next time Dawson went to see Freud, he invited him into the studio. "Oh boy, I was mesmerized! I was trying to take it all in so quickly, everything. For me it was the most remarkable room I had ever stepped into. The room is not huge but its size felt so human in scale and a large skylight flooded one half of the room with daylight.... On one big wooden easel sat a canvas, *Nude with Leg Up,* not finished ..."

Freud soon engaged Dawson, whose first task was to help take a portrait of Bindy Lambton, *Woman in a Butterfly Jersey* (1990–91), to his framer in Brick Lane. The canvas was wrapped in one of the many hotel sheets that served as paint rags, and stowed in Freud's old Bentley. Dawson recalls that Freud at the time was also working on other Bowery portraits. He always worked on four or five paintings at once, never mixing his day painting with his night painting (or his night models with his day models). And when he was not working on a canvas, it was turned to the wall. Tellingly, the studio door was always kept closed, keeping the space sacrosanct. "You always entered the studio and immediately this would give a different atmosphere, an atmosphere of trying to make something that's never been seen before, and personal and being fearless," Dawson said.

Besides the Bowery series, which tends to dominate Freud's oeuvre from the early to mid-1990s, paintings from the period include a portrait of Bruce Bernard (1992) standing by a pile of paint rags with downward gaze; *Two Women* (1992), whose slender, atypically lovely female forms are stretched on an iron bedstead; and a compact, upside-down nude, *Woman Holding Her Thumb* (Louise Liddell, his long-time framer). *Ib and Her Husband* (1992) shows a cozily cradled connubial pair; it is in stark contrast to the somber *And the Bridegroom,* done a year later.

These paintings were included in a major exhibit at the Whitechapel Art Gallery in London, *Lucian Freud: Recent Work,* which ran from September 10 to November 21, 1993. Despite its name, the exhibit ranged from work from the 1940s through the Leigh Bowery series, and Freud's recent naked self-portrait, on which he continued to work even after it was photographed for the catalogue. The comprehensive essay was written by the curator Catherine Lampert, who had also modeled for Freud. The show traveled to the Metropolitan Museum of Art from December 17, 1993 through March 15, 1994, before continuing to Madrid.

It had only been six years since the 1987 Freud retrospective was turned down by other American venues, before finally finding a place at the Hirshhorn. Now, with the Whitechapel show, Freud became, quite literally, the talk of the town. Lines formed to see the show at each stop. Freud had finally reached the rank of international art star, with all that such celebrity entailed.

Press on the show ranged from silly to serious. The *Balti-*

more Sun quipped: "London's latest and somewhat unlikely sexy
cultural hero is the 70-year-old grandson of Sigmund Freud, the
realist painter of people, Lucian Freud. His show of recent portraits and mostly naked figures at the Whitechapel Art Gallery
is the hottest ticket in town. Mr. Freud is not quite as big a draw
as Madonna, but he's had better reviews. And he's showing a lot
more frontal nudity." "Is This Man The Greatest Lover In Britain?" ran a front-page headline in the *Daily Mail*.

Michael Kimmelman reviewed the show in the *New York
Times* when it arrived at the Metropolitan Museum. Using by
now familiar terminology, he raved, "It leaves no doubt that,
at seventy-one, Mr. Freud is the greatest living figure painter."
Commenting on the Bowery portraits, he wrote, "Extravagance
of paint meets extravagance of flesh in a monumental way, and
the result is something weirdly beautiful . . ." And he singled out
the first Tilley painting: "What may be the most startling work
in the Metropolitan's exhibition, the just-completed *Evening in
the Studio,* casts a bird's eye view on a giant nude woman, a slender seamstress and a whippet. . . . It's hard to call such an image
seductive, but as with so many of his recent paintings, the se-
duction is in the handling of the pigment. . . . You may find this
and other paintings at the Metropolitan disturbing, maybe off-
putting, at first. But you would have to be completely immune
to the sensuous pleasures of painting to be unaffected by Mr.
Freud's art."

Freud's international success was due in great part to the fact
that he had a new art dealer, the New York–based William Acquavella, whose high-end gallery represented a number of blue-
chip artists and estates, including Georges Braque, Francis Bacon, Pierre Bonnard, Henri Matisse, Paul Cézanne, and Willem
de Kooning, among other nineteenth- and twentieth-century
masters. Acquavella was famous for an historic art deal he made
in 1990 when, in a joint-venture with Sotheby's, he purchased

the entire stock of the Pierre Matisse gallery for an estimated $153 million.

William Acquavella was born into the business; his father, Nicholas, had founded Acquavella Galleries in 1921. Although he comes across more like a business executive — he's known for his superb negotiating skills — than an art dealer, Acquavella has a casual elegance. Despite his success, he had a comfortable, unostentatious manner that may have reminded Freud of his many titled friends.

Acquavella had met the artist a few times through various friends in London, including a very close friend, David Somerset (chairman of Marlborough Fine Art and the 11th Duke of Beaufort, whom the artist painted); but when Freud first suggested having dinner, Acquavella tried to invent a good excuse. In 1992, he and his wife were persuaded to come to the Holland Park studio, where Acquavella promptly fell in love with the Leigh Bowery portraits. "I was sold," he recalls. He wasn't just sold, he bought the lot, most of which he sold to the collector Joe Lewis, and one to the publishing magnate Si Newhouse, holding back a few for other collectors, to "spread it around." The Metropolitan Museum bought *Naked Man, Back View*.

In the 2012 documentary, Acquavella vividly described first seeing the work. "He pulls out the first Leigh Bowery painting, which is Leigh Bowery's back and then he pulls out Leigh Bowery with the leg up and he pulls out one more Leigh Bowery in a red chair, and by the way, he does this all by himself and they're huge paintings. He doesn't want anybody touching them. I see these three paintings and I was absolutely taken by them, you know the monumentality of them. I thought they were so fabulous and I turned to my wife because I had been told before this by a lot of dealers and friends of mine in London that he was painting these male nudes and you know they are totally unsaleable, and you know he's difficult to deal with and all this kind of stuff. So anyway, I asked my wife, 'Do you think these are erotic paintings . . . ' and she said 'No,' and I said, 'Well I don't either. I think they're unbelievable.'"

The dealer told the artist, "If I can represent you worldwide, let's do it. . . . There's no contract, if it doesn't work for you, you tell me and we stop. And if it doesn't work for me, I'm gonna tell you, and we stop, it's over." Over dinner, Freud mentioned to Acquavella that he had a gambling debt that he wanted him to take care of. "So I said 'sure, no problem.' I mean what can it be, a gambling debt. So I met with the bookie and I said, 'I'd like to find out what Lucian owes.' And he said, 'that's wonderful, Bill, it's 2.7 million pounds.'"

In an interview for the *Wall Street Journal,* just months before his death in July, 2011, Freud praised Acquavella as "a gentleman." As he recalled it, "My dealer at the time was not as keen on the male nudes as I wanted him to be. . . . When William walked into the studio all the Leigh Bowery paintings were there; he was knocked out by them. You'd think a rather uptown, established gallerist would be slightly put off, but not a bit of it. He just thought these were remarkable paintings. We shook hands. It was that simple. We never looked back."

Both men greatly benefitted from the business partnership. "A lot," Freud succinctly stated when asked what contribution Acquavella had made to his global success. The two, who spoke on the telephone daily, also had, as Freud put it, "a real working friendship." The friendship included trips to Paris and Madrid on Acquavella's private jet. Acquavella also sat for Freud's portrait. "I sat for an intense period of a few weeks from three thirty to seven," he recalls. "Freud mixed a new color for every stroke."

Not Going Gently

F IVE YEARS AFTER they first met, Freud asked Da-vid Dawson to pose for him, beginning an ongoing series. The resulting work is *Pluto, Sunny Morning, Eight Legs* (1997). Like many of Freud's paintings, it started out as some-thing slightly different, depicting Dawson; Henrietta, a model Freud was currently using; and Freud's whippet, Pluto. "As the painting grew his interest and fixation ... became more and more about my connection with his whippet," Dawson recalled.

"I've always been aware, when he's been holding Pluto or I've used parts of him in paintings, that David would be good to work from as a whole. His presence and his appearance," Freud has said. He would paint Dawson and dog a number of times over the next decade or so; his assistant and his whippet, Eli, would be the subject of Freud's final, unfinished painting.

The composition could not be more quirky. Dawson, nude, lies on a sheet-covered bed, his arms around a small, graceful whippet curled against his side. A glimpse is seen of a window and a wardrobe. The bed with its reclining figures is front and center. But then there's a strangely humorous and surrealistic touch: a pair of legs, bent at the knee, can be seen protruding from under the bed (reminiscent of the protruding feet in *Two Men in the Studio*).

The legs are there as a compositional prop only; they came into play because the bottom of the canvas was vacant, and

Freud wanted to make it more lively. Dawson's trouser legs didn't suffice, so he proposed his bare legs. Lucian suggested Dawson playing his own double, and displaying his legs under the bed. "The spare legs came about out of desperation, as things quite often do in my pictures," Freud told Feaver. "The idea was to have in some way caught a scene rather than composed it, so that you never questioned it. I felt that the way I put things looked — not in a romantic way, I'd like to think — awkward, in the way that life looks awkward."

The "jokey" conceit somehow works. The legs beneath the bed face in the opposite direction of Dawson's similarly arranged legs on top of the bed. The dog fits into his body like a built-in appendage. It's a kind of jigsaw puzzle of living parts, all rather lovingly observed. This unlikely portrait of the artist's assistant with his dog somehow captures Freud's essence as an outlier.

Another quirky painting featuring Dawson (*Large Interior, Notting Hill* [1998]) caused a dispute with Mick Jagger and Jerry Hall, whom Freud had previously painted when Hall was eight months pregnant with her son, Gabriel. She was posing for a painting in which she is breast-feeding her son, but when she failed to show up for several sittings, Freud peremptorily replaced Hall's head with that of Dawson, creating the strange image of a man nursing a swaddled infant; in the foreground, an older man sits on a couch reading a book, a whippet curled at his feet.

"I was disappointed at first that it didn't work out with her," Freud said. "But in the end it didn't really matter to the painting. There was a certain quiet drama I thought about the original scene, and then with David as her replacement the drama got a bit louder."

Freud turned seventy-eight on the cusp of the millenium. Always a creature of habit, he now finally had money, and his daily routine outside the studio included a round of favorite restaurants he had been frequenting since the mid-to-late 1990s, when he could afford a more affluent lifestyle. There was Clarke's, owned by a friend, Sally Clarke, where he ate both breakfast (getting a milky "Mr. Freud latte" and large Danish) and lunch, usually shared with Dawson, and, in the evenings, Locanda Locatelli. He was a famous regular at The Wolseley, a posh bistro where Freud had a ringside table and was also quite friendly with its owner, Jeremy King. Over the next few years Freud did several paintings of both restaurateurs, including a portrait of King (2007) and a huge, beautiful etching plate that required over a hundred sittings and was never finished.

In May 2000, Freud had a date with Queen Elizabeth at the Royal Collection's Friary Court picture conservation studio in St. James Palace, where her majesty had agreed to pose for him. Freud completed the portrait in December, 2001; the final touch was the tiara he had requested she wear. She consented, but by the time Freud was ready to paint it, she was too busy to sit, so he used a stand-in model, squeezing the diamond tiara awkwardly into the top of the tiny canvas. The portrait proved highly controversial, sparking a number of cruel — and much-quoted — comments. In the *Times,* Richard Morrison remarked, "The chin has what can only be described as a six o'clock shadow and the neck would not disgrace a rugby prop forward. The expression is of a sovereign who has endured not one annus horribilis but an entire reign of them." Robert Simon, the *British Art Journal*'s editor, memorably commented: "It makes her look like one of the royal corgis who has suffered a stroke."

At seventy-nine, Freud was still actively pursuing women — at least some of whom eagerly reciprocated. In 2001, he began living with a twenty-seven-year-old journalist named Emily Bearn, who wrote a weekly column for the *Sunday Telegraph.* The artist was also rumored to have bought his latest muse a 500,000-pound sterling terraced house in West London. Freud painted her both clothed and naked: she appears in *Small Por-*

trait and *Daughter and Father,* both 2002. She's also the subject of several 2001 nudes, including one done entirely in tones of grey, her girlish pumps on the floor by a torn mattress. When their relationship ended, several years later, Freud reportedly showed up at the house late one night, furiously kicking the door and shouting. Bearn refused to let him in.

Freud had recently gotten in touch with his son by Jacquetta Eliot, Freddy, now twenty-nine, who appears in two odd pictures done in 2000. *After Cézanne,* based on *L'Aprés-midi à Naples,* is a picture of a brothel scene that Freud actually owned, although he didn't bring it to the studio as a reference. In it, a naked Freddy, lying on a rumpled sheet on the floor, leans on his elbow, one leg under the buttocks of Julie, a model Freud had met through Big Sue; another woman bears a tea-tray. A toppled chair adds to the sense of general disarray. In *Freddy* (2000–01) the lank frame of Freud's long-haired son is virtually backed into a corner of the studio.

In 2002, Freud painted another powerful self-portrait. Still painting day and night, the artist depicted himself as palpably frail. There is a tentative, tremulous feeling to this work that sets it apart. Surrounded — and almost absorbed by — an impressive impasto of brushstrokes on the wall, his face looks wistful, full of dark folds and shadows. Although he is wearing a jacket, he is shirtless, and one hand clutches his grey-blue cravat. The image exudes an unmistakable aura of finality.

"His face it's so tender, it's almost as if he had so much compassion for himself as a much more fragile person," his daughter Bella says in the 2012 documentary, her voice cracking with emotion. "And actually I thought he looked much more fragile in that painting than he did in real life."

In June 2002, the Tate mounted a major Freud retrospective of 150 works, from 1939 through 2002, including the recent self-portrait, completed just a month earlier — and one of a nude Emily Bearn. Perhaps it's a measure of Freud's status as a national treasure that the Tate agreed to the artist's demand that the galleries have only natural light. Two nights before the opening, Freud hosted a private view followed by a dinner for friends and models, a motley group who ranged from the Duke and Duchess of Devonshire and David Hockney to Freud's daughters Esther and Bella, to Sue Tilley, Kate Moss, and Bearn.

The mammoth show was curated by William Feaver, who had first started writing about Freud and his work in 1968. His extensive catalogue essay, "Freud: Life into Art," constituted a significant update on the saga recorded by Lawrence Gowing twenty years earlier, bringing new understanding and insight to a painter now widely considered to be a major twentieth-century artist. Woven into the text were a number of revealing comments made by Freud. The retrospective ran from June 20 through September 22, before traveling to the Fundació la Caixain in Barcelona from October 22 through January 12, 2003 and ending at the Museum of Contemporary Art, Los Angeles, from February 9 to May 25, 2003.

The Economist began its review by simply stating, "The paintings in the Lucian Freud retrospective at the Tate Britain have been acclaimed by critics as the work of a genius. They believe without reservation that Mr. Freud is the nation's greatest living painter. And in many ways he is. . . . Today Mr. Freud's painterly gravitas seems an increasingly valuable commodity in an age . . . where conceptual installation and video art attract ever more attention. . . . Yet Mr. Freud's work remains resolutely modern, depicting the human form as simple flesh, stripped of presence and protection, beautiful in its ugliness, reality laid bare."

The show opened at MOCA to reviews that were considerably more critical. In the *Los Angeles Times,* Christopher Knight wrote: " . . . all but a handful of more than a hundred paintings and eighteen works on paper are visual essays on the fascination and inevitable failure of the flesh. . . . Behold the man — and woman — his pictures say, again and again. He's ... routinely described — not least by the marketing machinery around this show — as Britain's greatest living figurative painter ... it may be true, but given the limited competition, its meaning is circumscribed. Freud is in reality a fine painter with a very narrow repertoire — and a tendency to manipulate the audience to dubious effect."

In 2002, *Tatler* named Freud, nearly eighty, the most eligible bachelor in Britain after Prince Harry. And Kate Moss went on the record as saying he was "the person she would most like to meet" in an interview in a magazine called *Dazed & Confused*. Moss also declared she was eager to pose for him. Lucian had danced with her once at a club, and was intrigued. He called his daughter Bella, and said "Can you send her around right away?" The artist invited the model to dinner. "I went to his house and he started [painting] that night. Couldn't say no to Lucian. Very persuasive. I phoned Bella the next day and said 'how long is it going to take?' She said, 'How big is the canvas?'" Moss recalled.

It took Freud nine months to paint the nearly life-size nude portrait of Moss, who was pregnant with her daughter Lila Grace at the time. Moss sat from seven in the evening until two in the morning, seven nights a week. Freud pronounced the painting "disappointing," although he said Moss was "physically intelligent" but "always late to her sittings." (It later sold for about $6.2 million.) But Moss will always have another original Freud: a pair of sparrows he tattooed just above her buttocks. It was a skill he learned during his short stint in 1941 with the Merchant Navy, when he used to improvise tattoos for the sailors, using India ink and a scalpel. When Moss first said she wanted an image of a bird, he showed her his 1944 work, *Chicken in a Bucket*. They agreed on a flock of birds, which became a pair.

That same year Freud and his fellow artist and friend David Hockney agreed to sit for each other. Most mornings in the summer of 2002, Hockney would walk from his studio through Holland Park, arriving at Notting Hill. He sat over a period of three months. Although Hockney sat for hours in a straight-backed chair, smoking and exchanging "bitchy artist gossip" with Freud, the finished portrait is a bust from the shoulders up, his collar open, his glasses perched on his nose. Hockney praised Freud's laborious method, saying, "you get to know and watch the face doing many things . . . looking and peering . . . coming closer and closer . . . his portraits are as good as has been done by anybody, photographs can't get near it."

Once he had completed his portrait of Hockney, Freud sat for him as agreed, arriving at his studio by Bentley. But even with Dawson by his side, he only managed to sit for three hours. Hockney did a double portrait of the artist and his assistant.

Freud's paintings from the 1990s on were huge, and often rather stagey. In order to produce them, the five-foot-six-inch artist usually stood on a set of steps to work on them. Such was the case with the six-foot-high painting of his friend Andrew Parker Bowles, with whom he often rode horses in Hyde Park, in typical risk-taking fashion refusing to wear a helmet. Parker Bowles was impressed with Freud's innate understanding of the animals.

In 2003, Freud began his grand portrait of Parker Bowles, dressed in his full uniform as a brigadier, from honorary medals to polished boots. Freud broke the formality of what would otherwise be a traditional British military portrait, done, say, by Gainsborough, by depicting Parker Bowles with his paunch bulging through his unbuttoned jacket. As Parker Bowles later said of *The Brigadier* (2003–4), "When I look in the mirror I think, not bad, but then I see the painting and hear people say things like, 'It shows the decline of the British Empire,' well, so be it."

In April 2004, Freud had a show of his work from the last two years at The Wallace Collection. It was a huge success: the normally uncrowded institution, was, says Annie Freud, "stuffed to the gunnels from morning to night." Reviewing the show in the *Guardian,* Robert Hughes emphatically wrote, "At 81, Freud is so much younger than any of the Britart dreck installed on the other side of the Thames; younger than Damien Hirst's slowly rotting shark in its tank of murky formalin; weirder than David Falconer's Vermin Death Star, which is composed of thousands of cast-metal rats, and about a hundred times sexier than Tracey Emin's stale icon of sluttish housekeeping, her much-reproduced bed."

In 2004, Freud did a now famous portrait of art critic Martin Gayford, *Man in a Blue Scarf,* which was the basis of Gayford's book, *Man with a Blue Scarf: On Sitting for a Portrait By Lucian Freud,* published in 2010, in which Gayford minutely chronicles their hundreds of sittings over a period of a year and a half for both the portrait and a later etching. During this time Freud did his fair share of chatting, and although he comes across as perhaps more of a sweet old man — as James Kirkman puts it, "Father Christmas" — than he actually was, the beautifully illustrated book offers rare, and often charming, insights into the artist at work in his sanctum.

At eighty-two, Freud continued to live up to his tabloid label of "Lothario." His latest lover was Alexandra Williams-Wynn, an art student and the daughter of a Welsh baronet, who began sitting for the artist at age thirty-two, after writing him a fan letter. The two soon became lovers. "I wasn't taking it serious at first — I was fully aware of the age difference," she told *Vanity Fair* nearly a decade later. "But I fell in love with him. It was sort of out of my hands."

Williams-Wynn was the subject of *Naked Portrait,* (2004–5). Freud's next astonishing painting, also featuring his current muse, was the last he would paint in the Holland Park studio, where the six flights of stairs had become a problem. His work from then on would be done in the studio at his home in Notting Hill, where the artist had bought a small Georgian house with a garden some years before.

The painting, entitled *The Painter Surprised by a Naked Admirer* (2004–5), is actually a portrait within a portrait: the caricature of an aging artist and his youthful partner. A stooped and clothed Freud stands in his studio, complete with the encrusted wall, the many paint rags on the floor, a tall stool holding brushes, and a glimpse of an easel that holds the same portrait — the naked Williams-Wynn clasping the leg of the barefooted artist, her hand on his thigh.

The convoluted painting took a year to complete — and when it ended, so did the relationship. Like many of his former female models, Williams-Wynn had a difficult time adjusting to the abrupt finish, her comments echoing those of Freud's lover Anne Dunn so many years before. As Williams-Wynn told *Vanity Fair,* "Being with Lucian made me realize that this is no joke: being an artist, being alive. It also made me understand that selfishness is what it takes to make great art."

Leaving the Studio

IN A CONCESSION to his advancing age, Freud had stopped using the Holland Park studio, but his output didn't dwindle. Over the next six years he produced an impressive number of paintings and etchings. Even Dawson marveled at "the sheer volume, the scale." Freud would only stop painting when it became physically impossible. He continued to push himself as hard as he could.

Asked about his stamina and focus, he told Feaver, "I think it's to do with what matters, and what I'm thinking about, and what I steer by . . . I'd rather not go completely absent-minded because small things to do with working really worry me and I want to get back and change them and adjust them, and then I forget what it is I wanted to change. Considering that I'm completely selfish and I only do what I want to do, what am I doing forgetting what I want to do. That's the worrying thing. . . ."

In 2005, Freud did a painting of William Acquavella, entitled *New Yorker in a Blue Shirt,* followed a year later by an etching with the same title.

He attempted his widest canvas to date, a large nude with a heavily impastoed face (*Ria, Naked Portrait,* 2006–7). Freud conceded to Feaver that at this point he could work a maximum of three and a half to four hours, adding, "I hope I can go on painting even when I can't stand up at it."

Some of the best and most moving images of the last years

of Freud's life are his portraits of David Dawson with various whippets — first Pluto, then Eli, whom Freud gave him as a gift in 2000. *David and Eli* (2003–4), first shown just after it was completed at the Wallace show, was singled out by Hughes as the exhibit's masterpiece. In it a nude Dawson is splayed on a bed, Eli languidly stretched by his side. *Eli and David* (2005–6) shows his assistant in an armchair, his dog lovingly curled in his lap. Freud's extraordinary affinity with animals is alive in the beautiful form of the dog, and its warmth extends to the image of a smiling Dawson. While the assistant's right hand and face are somewhat worked over, the painting has a looseness and ease about it; above all, it is imbued with affection.

In 2007, Freud had a major show at the Museum of Modern Art, *Lucian Freud: The Painter's Etchings,* which included some one hundred works and further cemented Freud's reputation in the twentieth-century canon. In the *New York Times,* Roberta Smith wrote: "Moving through its galleries, you may conclude that tough as Mr. Freud's paintings are, his etchings are somehow even starker, more raw and brutal. They bring the violence of his rendering style closer to the surface. Compared with the loamy explorations of Mr. Freud's paintings, the etchings might almost be X-rays. The best show us sides of the image, like scaffoldings that have been partly draped with nets — often hallucinatory patches of lines, gouges, hatching and crosshatching. The frenetic marks lead lives of their own while somehow also coalescing to imply flesh . . ."

Freud's compulsive work habits never really let up. At eighty-seven, he was still working almost round the clock. When Geordie Greig interviewed him for the *Evening Standard* in 2010, he asked the artist if he was still ambitious. "Yes, very," Freud replied. "I work every day and night. I don't do anything else. There is no point otherwise." Of old age, Freud said, "I think about avoiding death, keeping it at bay." "Are you still hungry for life?" Greig asked him. "I'm too lively not to be. I feel very active. I have been very lucky and my eyesight has always been good."

In April 2011, just a few months before his death, Freud finished his last female nude, a portrait of a young woman named Perienne Christian. They were close, but did not become lovers. As Christian told *Vanity Fair,* "He was extremely aware of running out of time, and wanting to do so much more." Martin Gayford, who saw him near the end, recalls, "He had cancer. It had been evident for some time. It had spread. It was clear a month or two before he died that he was going to die. He was getting very thin."

Freud's last painting was one that he had been working on for four years, another portrait of Dawson and Eli. He was still working on it just a few days before his death.

When he realized he was too frail to pick up a brush, Freud retreated to the bedroom of his Georgian house in Notting Hill, just above his studio. For several weeks before his death, close friends, intimates, and various children from his many relationships came to bid him goodbye, including Lady Jane Willoughby, one of his longest-term lovers. A number of his children were regular visitors. While Rose supervised much of his medical care, Esther and Bella, both of whom lived in London, were constant presences. And Annie, who lived outside London, also saw him frequently.

"I had been visiting Dad regularly, and I would go to the house and we would maybe have breakfast or go out to lunch," she recalls. "I would drop in to Clarke's restaurant — he would always be there for breakfast. As his illness became more serious, and he began to lose strength, I got regular bulletins about his state from other family members, and I saw him more frequently. There was a really, really special time once when I went there and he was really, really pleased to see me and feeling pretty low, and he said we couldn't go out but would I come upstairs. So we went upstairs and we lay down on the bed, and I kind of cuddled him, and it was really, really special. Because we didn't touch very often. Sometimes I might help him on with his coat, and he always kissed me when he greeted me and when I said goodbye. But actually kind of being physically close was something that hadn't happened in a very, very significant amount of time.

"He had painted the most beautiful painting of buttercups in the sixties, absolutely mind-blowingly beautiful. You know buttercups have that slightly greasy look. And I had brought him this massive bunch of buttercups, and he was so pleased. I put it in a vase in his room, and he said, 'Bring it closer where I could see it,' and that was so wonderful. I said, 'I wish I could do something to make you feel better.' And he immediately brightened as if to acknowledge somehow the importance of our relationship. Because we had had this really serious period of estrangement [in the early 1980s]. He said, 'Just you being here makes me feel better.' He said it as if it suddenly occurred to him as something that I really needed to hear. I could see that thought in his mind, 'What Annie really needs to know is that she is really important to me.' You could see that sort of what you might call emotional intelligence at work. It was a very poignant and wonderful moment."

Bella later recalled that they had had time to emotionally adjust to their father's impending death. "You know with my father, we all knew he was going to die. We were all preparing ourselves." Tragically, Bella and Esther's mother, Bernadine Coverley, died just four days after Lucian. "With Dad dying we thought we would be able to talk to her about the past, and we didn't," she has said. "But it's weird, in a funny way, my parents left us really strong. It was something to do with them being each in their own way true to themselves and insistent on the way they did things, and also sort of being funny and nice as well."

The artist Jane McAdam Freud also spent some meaning-

ful time with her father during his last days — and created several portraits of him. It was Bella who had first put Jane back
in touch with Lucian when Jane was in her early thirties, after
seeking her out when both young women were in Rome, and
later arranging a meeting with their father in London. Since
then, Jane had remained in intermittent contact with her father.
"We had a relationship. We wrote to each other. I saw him on
and off. I taught portrait drawing in Portobello Road, which
was very close to where the studio in Holland Park was, and he
used to drink in the pub, so I'd see him in that pub during that
period."

Jane had actually first done a sculpture of Lucian in 1991,
spending over a year to complete it; at that time, he also worked
on one of her. In 2001, she was commissioned to make a portrait on a medallion and asked her father to sit for her again. He
told her, "Oh, they will think I'm vain. It would be better to do
it later — when it makes sense as a memento mori." But when
he became mortally ill, he agreed. In addition to the medallion,
she produced a large double-sided terra-cotta relief (*EarthStone
Triptych*), imprinted copper coins, and a number of sketches, all
later displayed in a 2012 show at the Freud Museum, her great-
grandfather's one-time house. "I don't want to talk about the
death things.... He wanted to see me. I'd never seen a face light
up that much when I came into the room the first time. Very expressive."

Several other of Lucian's offspring, who had only seen the
priapic and self-described "absentee" patriarch once or twice
since they were infants, found a last-minute opportunity to say
goodbye. Jane's younger brother David, who had not seen his
father since the 1980s, when he enlisted Lucian's financial help
with his mother, Katherine, also proved himself to be Lucian's
progeny by producing art in response to his imminent death.
David spent a few days drawing by his father's deathbed, later

using the sketches to create a group of portraits, which he exhibited. "I felt he was more mine when he had died. I was able to digest him without barriers. He was more available to me," David has said.

Another McAdam sibling, Lucy, who also makes art, was shocked to learn that her father, whom she hadn't seen since her twenties, was dying. "I know he hadn't been very well but I didn't know he was that ill." She recalls a day towards the end: "I was sitting at the end of the bed. We were kind of touching one another, and he was stroking my arm. He was being as affectionate as could be and I showed him a picture of my sons, and I said, 'These are your grandchildren.' He was really staring at me, so much that I thought he went into some trance. It seemed like a frozen moment, and then I said, 'You can have it if you like,' he seemed to be so absorbed in it, and he said, 'Oh, can you put it under my pillow?' So I put it under the pillow and he said, 'No, no, not like that, with a bit showing so I can get it out.'" When Lucy told him she had to leave because she had promised to take some special-needs children she worked with to the theater, he asked her to come back later. "I would have done anything in the world to have heard that, but I don't want to ever let people down in my life, maybe because I've always been let down in my life, and I had to keep my promise," she says. It was the last time she saw him.

When Lucian Freud died of bladder cancer on July 20, 2011, at age eighty-eight, he was surrounded by some of his many children. Bella, Esther, Rose, Susie, and "quite a lot of us, all gathered at the house," says Annie. "I saw him dead, we all did." The night after Freud's death, his corner table at the Wolseley was draped in black; a single candle was lit in his honor.

A private funeral was held on July 27. It was officiated by the former archbishop of Canterbury, Rowan Williams, Celia Paul's brother-in-law and a close family friend. "It was a beautiful service," says Annie. "Many family members contributed either a eulogy or poem. We sang some hymns and then we proceeded to the grave."

Lucian Freud was laid to rest in Highgate Cemetery. In a coda he himself might have scripted, a horse (one of his earliest inspirations — his first serious work of art was a three-legged horse) was present at his burial: Sioux, a local horse that Freud had befriended and painted, accompanied the funeral procession to his grave.

In his studio, which had been left untouched, Lucian Freud's last unfinished portrait was still sitting on his easel. The huge painting portrayed two of his favorite subjects, a naked human — his devoted assistant David — and a dog, Dawson's whippet, Eli. The size of the canvas, entitled *Portrait of the Hound*, was a stark reminder of the scope of Lucian Freud's ambition, one he realized during his lifetime, of becoming perhaps the greatest realist painter of the twentieth century.

"That's the last [bit] Lucian was working on, around Eli's head, and beginning to put the shoulder in. One of the last marks he made was just his ear, where he just put two brushstrokes and suddenly you know Eli's listening to you," Dawson has said. Despite his age, the artist's decisions were "as ambitious as ever," according to his assistant.

"He put two extensions on this painting, because the way he painted my arms . . . stretching right down the canvas, it needed more space around it, so he added another four or five inches onto this side, and then again as my foot and knee came down the canvas, that needed space, so he's put another eight or nine inches at the bottom, and that's how he built up the canvas. Really it was dictated by the forms within the body. . . . But again he spent many, many days lightening the left-hand corner, and darkening the right-hand corner, and that took as much time and decision-making as it would painting how my knee wraps around my elbow. He would spend as much time looking at the floorboards. He always wanted you in the room, even if he was working on an area that had nothing to do with it. Because it did affect the painting."

You can sense the ebb of Freud's remarkable energy in the figure of Dawson, more thinly painted than usual, as if Freud's famously intense focus had faltered. And the painting is particularly poignant because Freud never began putting in Eli's hind legs, where a blank white space signals the artist's final absence, serving as a kind of epitaph.

But even unfinished, Freud's final portrait is a testament to his extraordinary sensibility as a painter. Of what he expected of great art, he had once said, "I ask it to astonish, disturb, seduce, convince." All of which, to one degree or another, Lucian Freud's work does.

Acknowledgments

Lucian Freud is a notoriously difficult subject to write about, from his famous pedigree to his personal life to the work itself. His extreme penchant for privacy (and the people in his life who helped enforce it) discouraged all biographers during his lifetime; indeed, in the early 1990s one writer was so intimidated by the alleged threats he received that he not only abandoned his project but also left London, at least for a time. Not long after that, *Vogue* magazine was forced to retract an entire feature article it had published on Freud; further, the author was asked to destroy all her research.

Even after his death, Freud's immediate circle has remained for the most part closemouthed. So it is with great gratitude that I wish to acknowledge those people who agreed to be interviewed for this book. They include, not in alphabetical order, Annie Freud, Carola Zentner, Jane McAdam Freud, Lucy McAdam Freud, David McAdam Freud, John Richardson, Martin Gayford, Sandy Nairne, Francis Outred, Volker M. Welter, Nancy Schoenberger, Anthony d'Offay, James Kirkman, James Demetrion, Dania Jekel, Sophie Freud, and Sue Tilley.

Although I did not formally interview him, I would also like to thank William Acquavella for meeting with me at the outset of this project. Although it was not possible for me to interview David Dawson, I want to thank him as well for his quick responses to my requests during my visit to London in February 2012, where I met him at the opening of the National Portrait Gallery's record-breaking retrospective *Lucian Freud: Portraits,* and for his revealing photographs of Freud at work in his studio, which I saw when they were shown at the Hazlitt Holland-Hibbert gallery in London.

This book could not have been written without the support of my friends, including Patricia Cohen, Mark Moore, Lorraine Monchak, Josephine Schmidt, Linda Eckstein, Jonathan Greenberg, Kathleen McAuliffe, Kim Uchiyama, Gwenda Blair, Claudia Doring-Baez, Alejandro Baez-Sacasa, Emma McCagg, Raul Zamudio, Mark Tansey, Miela Ford, and Dennis Kardon, whose generous loan of reference books from his personal library was indispensable to me. Thanks also to Sara Goff for her hospitality in London, to Annalyn Swan for her encouragement, and to Phyllis Schimel for her support throughout. And, of course, this book could not have happened without the editor of the Icons series, James Atlas, whose immediate enthusiasm for the project got it off the ground.

Bibliography

No writer attempting to research the life and work of Lucian Freud could get very far without the following books, catalogues, and films, all of which are helpful, and some of which are key, to understanding the man and his work.

Lawrence Gowing, himself an artist, as well as a curator and prominent art writer, wrote the first comprehensive monograph on Freud, whom he originally met in 1938 and followed closely for years. *Lucian Freud,* published by Thames and Hudson in 1982, is a richly illustrated book that offers intelligent and invaluable insights on the artist and his work; it is an excellent Freud primer.

Bruce Bernard's enormous eponymous tome on Freud, designed by Derek Birdsall and published by Random House in 1996, offers incisive critical perceptions in a 23-page introductory essay to the book's 290 lavish full-page color plates, taking the trajectory of Freud's work through the mid-1990s. Bernard was a personal friend of Freud's who also photographed him extensively, including a series of striking images of the artist in his studio that appear in the book *Freud at Work,* published by Alfred A. Knopf in 2006, along with shots by David Dawson and an engaging full-length interview with Freud by Sebastian Smee.

John Russell's thoughtful catalogue essay for Freud's first Hayward Gallery show in 1974 (the essay was later excerpted in a catalogue for the Robert Miller Gallery show *Lucian Freud:*

Early Works in 1993) elegantly captures the spirit and sensibility of the artist's work.

Robert Hughes's landmark essay "Lucian Freud Paintings" introduces the well-illustrated catalogue (published by Thames and Hudson in 1987) produced in conjunction with a traveling show organized by the British Arts Council, which opened at the Hirshhorn Museum in Washington, D.C., before going to Berlin, Paris, and London's Hayward Gallery. Few contemporary art writers are as canny and quotable as Hughes, who also includes in his text a number of memorable comments from Freud.

William Feaver has focused his art-historical and curatorial eye on Freud for decades, producing two of the best texts ever written on the artist. His exhaustive and edifying essay "Lucian Freud: Life into Art," written for the catalogue of the Freud retrospective at the Tate Britain in 2002, is a must-read for anyone interested in Freud. In addition to Feaver's own expertise on his subject, the essay includes biographical material on Freud's life and personal relationships, as well as a number of remarkable comments by the artist himself. Feaver later used much of this material in the 37-page introductory essay for his Rizzoli book *Lucian Freud*, which includes 362 full-page color plates as well as four interviews with the artist conducted in 1992, 1998, 2001, and 2007.

Catherine Lampert wrote the essay for the catalogue of the 1993 show *Lucian Freud: Recent Work* at the Whitechapel Gallery, which later traveled to the Metropolitan Museum of Art in New York City, where it was a huge hit, before going to the Museo Nacional Centro de Arte Reina Sofia in Madrid. She is one of the few women to write about Freud, an artist often accused of misogyny, and her understanding of Freud and his work is psychologically astute.

Man with a Blue Scarf, published by Thames and Hudson in 2010, is art critic Martin Gayford's charming, chatty, anecdotal account of sitting for over a year for a portrait and an etching by Freud. Engagingly written and nicely illustrated, it is a popular addition to the existing Freud literature. This firsthand account gives the reader a vivid — if somewhat kind and gentle — sense of a real-time close encounter with Freud.

Little has been written about Lucian Freud's parents, Ernst and Lucie Freud; Volker M. Welter's book *Ernst L. Freud, Architect,* published by Berghahn Books in 2012, offers a wealth of well-researched material on Ernst Freud, his work, and the Berlin milieu into which Lucian was born. The chapter notes are particularly rich in references to secondary sources, including material by Sigmund Freud and his circle.

The Rare and the Beautiful, by Cressida Connolly (daughter of editor and critic Cyril Connolly, an early supporter of Freud's), tells the tale of the Garman sisters, who "captured the heart of Bohemian London." Lorna was the most beautiful of the sisters and it was she who first captured Lucian Freud's heart; he would later marry her niece Kitty Garman. Connolly gives a detailed account of the relationship between Lorna and Lucian, including the rivalry with her other lover, poet Laurie Lee, and of Lorna's role as an inspired muse: it was she who gave him a much-prized possession, a stuffed zebra head, and she who brought him the bird that led to his beautiful painting *Dead Heron.*

Nancy Schoenberger's biography of Lady Caroline Blackwood, *Dangerous Muse,* published by Nan A. Talese/Doubleday in 2001, is a highly readable narrative about a remarkable woman who turned out to be somewhat more than a match for Freud. In addition to a dramatic account of Freud's relationship with Blackwood, it provides well-researched background on the Soho social and cultural scene, as well as on Freud's relationship with Francis Bacon. It's stuffed with juicy tidbits and quotes, and its chapter notes include references to excellent secondary source material. (Three useful biographies of Francis Bacon are those by Michael Peppiatt, Andrew Sinclair, and Daniel Farson; also interesting on the Soho circle are Daniel Farson's *Soho in the Fifties* and his profile of Freud in *Sacred Monsters,* and memoirs *High Diver* by Michael Wishart and *Anything Once* by Joan Wyndham.)

Ivana Lowell, Lady Caroline Blackwood's daughter, wrote a memoir, *Why Not Say What Happened?*, published by Alfred A. Knopf in 2010. Although some of the anecdotes about Caroline and Lucian have been published elsewhere, Ivana's book offers personal insights into her mother and her stepfather, the poet Robert Lowell, who was Blackwood's third husband. It also goes into her mother's relationships with the legendary editor Robert Silvers and her second husband, composer Israel Citkowitz, who Ivana assumed was her father; it turned out to be Ivan Moffat, a screenwriter with whom her mother had had an affair. (In a piece Ivana wrote for the *Daily Beast* pegged to her memoir, she said that when she was fifteen years old, Lucian asked her to lunch and then to pose for him. When she told this to Lady Caroline, her mother said, "You are *never* going to sit for him. Don't you know he fucks everyone he paints?" More shockingly, she wrote that her older sister, Natalya, who later died of a drug overdose, claimed to have slept with Lucian.)

Although Clement Freud and Lucian Freud were famously estranged, Clement's memoir, *Freud Ego,* published by BBC Worldwide Limited in 2001, provided useful information regarding family background, including the three Freud boys' childhood in Berlin, experience at Dartington, and wartime days in London.

Two other books on Freud were also helpful. Sebastian Smee provides a good overview of Freud's work in *Lucian Freud: Beholding the Animal,* published by Taschen in 2009. Freud took a personal liking to Smee, a talented Australian art critic who now writes for the *Boston Globe;* he did a lengthy interview with Freud for the book *Freud at Work*, published by Knopf in 2006, which features striking photographs by both Bruce Bernard and David Dawson. (Smee himself is interviewed about the artist in Randall Wright's documentary, *Painted Life*.)

Two recent catalogues were also of great use:

Lucian Freud: The Studio, the catalogue produced for the Freud exhibit at the Centre Pompidou in 2010, includes a half dozen somewhat scholarly essays, and dramatically printed quotes from Freud break up its many color plates; it also offers a particularly comprehensive chronology of the artist's life.

Freud started out as a draughtsman before becoming a painter, and his skill at drawing underpins all of his work. *Lucian Freud Drawings* was published in 2012 by Acquavella Galleries in conjunction with Blain/Southern to accompany an extraordinary show of Freud's drawings that traveled from London to New York. The beautifully produced book includes 130 plates, spanning Freud's career, as well as an introduction by William Feaver and an essay by Mark Rosenthal on New York's somewhat slow-to-evolve appreciation of the artist.

Finally, the beautiful catalogue that accompanied the National Portrait Gallery's seminal retrospective *Lucian Freud: Portraits*, which ran from February 9 to May 27, 2012, and was its most popular paying art exhibit ever, includes essays by John Richardson and by curators Sarah Howgate and Michael Auping, in addition to 131 plates, a conversation between Auping and Freud done in sessions between May 2009 and January 2011, and a nicely illustrated chronology. The accompanying audio app to the National Portrait Gallery show is replete with comments from Freud's sitters, including family and friends, and is interspersed with statements made by the artist.

Two documentaries, *Lucian Freud: Portraits* by Jake Auerbach (produced in 2002) and *Lucian Freud: Painted Life* by Randall Wright (produced in 2012), are essential to a well-rounded view of Freud. Jake Auerbach, the artist Frank Auerbach's son, was able to get many of Freud's sitters, including

family, friends, and lovers, to speak frankly about the artist and
his work. *Lucian Freud: Painted Life,* which was broadcast on
the BBC in February 2012 in conjunction with the National
Portrait Gallery show (it was reedited and released as a DVD,
Freud's Naked Truths, when the gallery retrospective traveled to
the Modern Art Museum of Fort Worth, Texas, in July), is more
hard-hitting, providing a sometimes harshly honest portrayal
of the famously difficult artist. Both films include moving comments from several of Freud's daughters; *Painted Life* includes
rare footage of Freud painting in his studio, just a day or so before he died.

Illustration Credits

Freud with his grandfather, by unknown photographer, 1938, collection Bourgeron/RA/Le Brecht Music & Arts

Lucian Freud, by Walker Evans, circa 1950s, the Metropolitan Museum of Art, Walker Evans Archive, 1994 (1994.252.82.1-12)/Art Resource/copyright Walker Evans Archive, the Metropolitan Museum of Art

Lorna Wishart and Lucian Freud, by Francis Goodman, circa 1945, (film negative)/copyright National Portrait Gallery, London

Caroline Blackwood, by Walker Evans, circa 1950s, the Metropolitan Museum of Art, Anonymous Gift, 1999 (1999.246.115)/Art Resource/copyright Walker Evans Archive, the Metropolitan Museum of Art

Hotel Bedroom, Lucian Freud, 1954, (oil on canvas)/Beaverbrook Art Gallery, Fredericton, N.B., Canada/copyright the Lucian Freud Archive/the Bridgeman Art Library

Girl with a Kitten, Lucian Freud, 1947, (oil on canvas)/Private Collection/copyright the Lucian Freud Archive/the Bridgeman Art Library

Kitty Freud (Garman/Godley) with Annie, by unknown photographer (photo), circa 1948, the Beth Lipkin Archive, the New Art Gallery, Walsall, UK

Francis Bacon and Lucian Freud, by Harry Diamond, 1974, (vintage bromide print) copyright National Portrait Gallery, London

Lucian Freud with his mother, Lucie, by David Montgomery, circa 1980, (photo) Getty Images

The Painter's Mother Resting I, Lucian Freud, 1975–76, (oil on canvas) copyright the Lucian Freud Archive/the Bridgeman Art Library

Reflection (Self-Portrait), Lucian Freud, 1985, (oil on canvas)/Private Collection/copyright the Lucian Freud Archive/the Bridgeman Art Library

Working at Night, by David Dawson, 2005, (photo)/Private Collection/the Bridgeman Art Library

Index